Tales from the Animal Hospital

Tales from the Animal Hospital

David Grant

SIMON & SCHUSTER
A VIACOM COMPANY

First published in Great Britain by Simon & Schuster, 1997
A Viacom Company

Simon & Schuster
West Garden Place
Kendal Street
London W2 2AQ

Simon & Schuster of Australia
Sydney

A CIP catalogue record for this book is available
from the British Library.

0-684-82134-6

Printed and bound in Great Britain by
Butler & Tanner Ltd, Frome and London

For my father

Author's Note

Although all the stories that feature in this book are true, the names of pet owners have been changed to preserve their privacy.

CONTENTS

INTRODUCTION

The operation was practically over. It had gone well. The little old cat lying prone under the anaesthetic had come into the consulting room just over two weeks earlier. She had been eating her owner out of house and home, and drinking much more than usual, but she had lost weight. It didn't take long to make a diagnosis: she was suffering from hyperthyroidism, caused by the thyroid glands producing too much of their hormone. A blood sample confirmed this – her thyroxine levels were sky high – and I had elected to remove the overactive gland. The disease has been discovered in cats only relatively recently, and the operation – thyroidectomy – cures it successfully.

The last stitch went in and I stepped back to check the patient. Clunk! A blunt object delivered a hard blow to the back of my head. I looked round. It was a hand-held camera whose operator, Barry, just managed to keep his balance among the pile of cables on the floor. And Rolf Harris was grinning at me from the other side of the operating table. 'Mind your head, David,' he said But it wasn't my head I was worried about, it was the camera – some fifty thousand pounds' worth – not to mention Barry.

For ten minutes, while I'd been absorbed in the intricacies of the operation, I had forgotten I was being filmed. To the right of Rolf were two more enormous cameras on stands, with their operators behind them. Above me, attached to the operating light, another one focused on the site of the operation, and I was also being watched by the producer, two 'riggers', who would sort out any technical problems, a lighting specialist and a sound man. Plus there were a couple of monitors, which I had resisted the temptation to look at. It wasn't hard – they were a complete put off. And today, just to add to it all, another crew from *Points of View* were filming their colleagues. But I had forgotten all this – at least, temporarily. I was surprised at how easy it had been to adjust to their presence. A year earlier I had been working happily as the director of the RSPCA Harmsworth hospital and the idea of appearing in a popular television programme had never entered my head.

One day during the summer of 1994 Fiona Holmes of the BBC telephoned me. She was researching an idea that had come from the Science and Features Department. They had been having great success with their medical programmes, especially *Hospital Watch* which had struck a chord with the public, and were thinking of following this up with a programme about an animal hospital. Fiona had produced many quality science documentaries and has a sharp eye for what constitutes 'good television'. She had visited several veterinary establishments before that Monday morning when she arrived at Harmsworth to interview me.

Several film crews had visited us in recent years to shoot either one-off documentaries or news items and I had learnt how invasive television could be. On the other hand, though, there was no better way to get animal-welfare messages across to the public and to tell people about the RSPCA's work and I was keen to go ahead. Fiona was amazed at how busy we were and emphasised all the drawbacks – which only made me all the keener to give it a go.

Over the next three weeks Fiona and I had several meetings to talk about potential technical difficulties – such as where the OB (outside broadcast) units could be parked, and she was particularly concerned about the disruption to our working routines and whether we would be able to cope. After much thought on both sides, however, the Harmsworth was chosen for the programme. Filming would start in six weeks' time. What had I let us in for?

Animal Hospital was to be a live programme,

running every day for a week in late August or early September, broadcast at 7.30 p.m. – which meant we would be exposed to a prime-time television audience. The multi-talented Rolf Harris would present it. The critics had no idea what to expect: there were no previews and since the programme would be live they had no material by which to judge it. One said he hoped enough material would walk through the hospital door or Rolf 'would have to get his didgerydoo out'! The number of animals coming in was the least of our problems, though, because the hospital is almost always too busy. At least we could guarantee a continuous supply of interesting material.

In spite of all the careful explanations we had received, nothing could quite prepare us for the disruption once the filming started. I realised after the first few hours with the cameras how blasé I had become to life in the hospital when I saw the reactions of the BBC team to what I regarded as routine. At first the cameras were rolling all the time but then the producers learned to be more selective and we suddenly found ourselves developing strategies to make it less stressful.

We also had to get used to the fact that the number of people working in the hospital nearly doubles when the BBC team arrives. The board room, usually used for receiving VIPs, is taken over by monitors, phones, fax machines, and becomes a production office. The producers sit there during filming and issue instructions to the presenters and the director, all of whom are linked up by a system called talk-back. This amused me at first: a presenter or floor manager would break off a conversation and appear to be talking to themselves. The microphones are tiny, hidden in their ears, and there is a constant to and fro of information of which the rest of us who are not linked up are unaware.

The first series consisted of two weeks of filming. The first was a dummy run, the second was for real. Each night's programme consisted of the events of that day and included live operations and emergencies as they happened. It was a dramatic week, with a cruelty case that shocked viewers: a dog had been thrown off a balcony and died in the midst of attempts to save him. Another had to be put down, and his weeping owner was comforted by Rolf, who was also in tears.

The BBC had hoped for around three million viewers over the first week – that would be a more than satisfactory number for a new show – but we attracted around ten million. It was obvious that the public wanted more and a whole new concept for a television series had been born. Since then there have been one and sometimes two series every year and, so far, no signs of a fall in interest. Most aspects of the RSPCA's work have been treated – the vets and nurses in the hospital, of course, the inspectors, the homing centres, the wild-life hospitals and the ambulance service – and *Animal Hospital* coveys an accurate insight into the everyday life of all those working in the field for the RSPCA.

Despite all our careful preparations, though, there was one thing we hadn't thought about: television fame. Once the programme had gone out we had some adjusting to do to deal with the enormous increase in people coming to the hospital. It built up gradually during the first week of live broadcasts and suddenly we had people arriving from all over the place. Later we had to make it clear that we have a defined catchment area because, after all, there is a limit to the number of animals six vets can see in a day. Once the last programme had gone out I thought naively that pretty soon we would be back to normal. On the following Monday morning, though, there was an urgent knock on my office door. It was Chris, the receptionist: 'Have you seen downstairs, DG?' The waiting room was jammed. We can see a maximum of forty-five patients in a morning session – and by 9.30 we already had had far more than that. Then I looked out of the front door: a queue of more than a hundred people stretched down the road. I was aghast.

There was only one thing for it – I had to tell them that we couldn't see them all. Dressed in my theatre kit I went down the line explaining that we could handle only life-threatening emergencies and that we already had more than double the usual numbers. Some pet owners accepted this, others were angry and a few pleaded to be seen. It was surprising that so many healthy-looking animals seemed suddenly at death's door!

It took half an hour to sort out the queue and restore some semblance of order. At the end I was confronted by a youth with a skinny Staffordshire bull terrier. 'Dave, Dave, mate!' he shouted. I looked round for his friend, before realising that he was talking to me. 'I only want to see the nurses, I don't need a vet,' he went on. I couldn't help wondering about his motives, but I explained that nurses can only treat animals under supervision and that his dog would have to see a vet first.

The general mayhem went on for another two weeks and it was to be more than a month before we were back to normal. Curiously, we have experienced exactly the same rush of business and 'cooling down' period after each of the subsequent series, so at least we have learned that television fame is very short-lived – unless you are Rolf, who is part of TV history.

Over the past few years, we have seen many remarkable cases, but perhaps the one that stands out for me as typical both of the show and of our work at the hospital was Snowy. I have been involved with dozens of cruelty cases: some have made me angry, others have driven me to despair and virtually all of them have made me very sad. But I have never seen such a neglected animal as Snowy and to this day I can't understand how anyone could allow a pet to reach such a state. The RSPCA inspector, John Bowe, who dealt with the case, felt the same.

When Snowy was first brought to the hospital it was hard to believe she was a dog – she looked more like a bag of bones. Bairbre O'Malley, the experienced vet who examined her, could not fully take in what she was seeing. Even several years with the RSPCA and more in private practice had not prepared her for this. That it was a small dog she was examining was the only certainty. What hair remained on Snowy hung in loose cords, her underlying skin was inflamed and Bairbre said later that, after clipping, the dog looked like a pink pig. She was furiously itchy, scratching away throughout the examination, and, although it was impossible to say at this stage what breed she was, she appeared to be half the weight she should have been. Worse was to follow: to begin Bairbre thought Snowy was very old but when she looked at the dog's teeth, she discovered that this was a young dog of perhaps eighteen months or two years. How on earth could she have got into such a state?

The answer to this question was not immediately apparent. She had been abandoned with the police who, horrified, had called in the RSPCA ambulance service. Snowy had been picked up late at night. Bairbre's examination suggested a diagnosis, which was confirmed by skin scraping: not only was Snowy emaciated, she had scabies, which is a disease caused by tiny mites called *Sarcoptes scabiei.* They cause the terrible itching poor Snowy was experiencing and which she would have been suffering for at least three months. Yet scabies, once diagnosed, is easily treated with shampoos. What Snowy needed was a cure for the scabies, tender loving care, good food and a new owner. We resolved to make sure she got the lot.

We clipped her hair and gently bathed her in a shampoo to kill the mites. The tender loving care and good food came next: Snowy was so miserable that at first she shivered in the corner of her cage, refused to eat and could hardly raise her head. Here was a challenge for the nurses. Not long after beginning treatment they managed to get a little food down her – and then came the first hint of a tail wag.

When the story went out on television, the phones went mad. Everyone wanted Snowy. For a time the switchboard could not cope and in later programmes we pleaded with viewers not to phone the hospital but to use Ceefax to get information on particular cases.

Snowy made rapid progress and as soon as the itching subsided her appetite came back with a vengeance. Over the next three weeks her weight doubled. There was still some doubt as to her breed but she had begun to look like a poodle or, perhaps, a Bedlington terrier – only time would tell. Meanwhile John Bowe had selected a foster owner, a friend called Gordon: although Snowy was getting all the care in the world in the hospital she would really thrive in a proper loving home – probably the first she had ever known. Sure enough, with Gordon, Snowy soon blossomed into a self-confident, happy character. I was amazed yet again at how forgiving of humans a dog can be. Sadly, some dogs are so traumatised by cruel, thoughtless people that they never really recover. If you take on a dog with this sort of history, you will need tremendous reserves of patience and determination and some insight into dog psychology, particularly the effects of neglect and suffering. As these dogs have never learned to socialise with humans, they need the kind of training that they should have had in puppyhood.

Snowy turned out to be a poodle – and Gordon cannot go down the street without strangers recognising her and stopping him for a chat. The original owners not surprisingly, have never come forward, and despite all the publicity no one has told us who they were, which is a shame because it would be a special bonus to prosecute them. Plenty of people have tried to claim Snowy, saying she went missing, but always the proof was lacking, the photographs didn't match and Snowy showed no recognition – an important point, since dogs have long memories. When I was a student our family dog, Judy, was at my side whenever I was home from university. After my first seven years as a vet I spent a year in Colombia. On my return I was met by my parents at Heathrow with an ecstatic Judy, who refused to leave my side. She was one of the main reasons I came back earlier than I intended – I missed England, my folks and my dog!

Eventually Gordon and his wife adopted Snowy as she had settled in so well with them and she has not had a day's illness since. She is still a celebrity and I often see photos of her and Gordon opening fêtes or other charity events.

CHAPTER ONE

Doing the Rounds

I have spent almost half of my professional life working at the Harmsworth and a lot of my colleagues in the hospital or in charge of the clinics have spent several years working for the RSPCA. In fact, the three clinic managers associated with our group between them have nearly ninety years' experience and service. There is always a buzz about the place, often a drama, and what you see on television is unscripted, unrehearsed and barely edited.

The RSPCA Sir Harold Harmsworth Hospital, to

give it its full title, was built in 1968 with a legacy from Sir Harold, although the RSPCA pay the running costs. Sir Harold was a member of the publishing family and, when he died, he owned the *Field* magazine. He was an animal lover who wanted to ensure that pet owners in the poorer areas of north London, who were unable to afford private veterinary services, could have their animals treated. At that time the hospital was the most modern in Europe and quickly became one of the busiest – which it still is today.

I first worked at the hospital in 1971, staying for three happy and eventful years as a house surgeon, and returned in 1987, this time as its director, and I haven't had a dull moment since. It's impossible to be bored at the Harmsworth, although a little tedium might be welcome on those days when we are all rushed off our feet and the operating lists are huge.

My working day usually starts around 8.15 a.m., when I check the mail. One aspect of my job that escapes the cameras is the paperwork that mounts up – I could easily spend half the week doing administration but I try to fit it into lunch hours and coffee breaks. I have to deal with budgets, compile statistics for my bosses at the RSPCA headquarters and innumerable phone calls. We get hundreds of letters from people wanting advice – and never more than when the cameras are rolling. Many concern matters best left to the owner's vet, who is always the best judge in any individual case and will be happy to get a second opinion on a difficult case.

Then I'm ready to set out on my ward rounds. This

can take an hour and a half, since we may have up to a hundred animals resident at a time. I am accompanied by a reports nurse, who takes notes on an animal's progress to read to the owners when they phone in. Hopefully I will find many of the pets are fit to go home, where they are often better off, but those on drips or who are unable to stand have to stay. I've never been filmed on my ward rounds, I suppose because the logistics of trailing round the cameras and sound equipment are too much to overcome, but also the BBC team aim to be as non-invasive as possible.

My first ports of call are wards one and two, the main dog wards, which accommodate twenty dogs each. There are cages on one side of each ward, some of which are quite large, making them suitable for Great Danes and similar breeds. The majority are for small to medium-sized dogs and they are arranged in two tiers above each other. By the time I arrive the nurse is already hard at work. Each dog has to be fed and watered twice daily, its drugs administered and its cage cleaned. They are all taken outside twice daily to the dog run at the back of the hospital. Everything is written down in detail: which food was offered, whether or not it was eaten, and any problems such as vomiting or diarrhoea. The wards are kept at a pleasant temperature, winter and summer, as it is so important that sick dogs feel comfortable, especially after operations when the body temperature drops.

The dog wards can be noisy. Often an excitable animal will bark and set all the others off. We provide ear mufflers when things get too bad and there are some days when I can't wait to get out, especially after a night of broken sleep! Fortunately for the nurses, they rotate around the wards so none of them has to put up with the racket for too long.

After a week, a nurse will usually have bonded with any long-term stayers and vice versa. Sometimes after only three or four days the most intransigent, aggressive or frightened dog will be like a lamb with his favourite nurse. In serious road accident cases, which we see commonly, and with advanced or complicated medical conditions, dedicated nursing makes all the difference to the speed of a dog's recovery.

This was certainly true of Beth, a little Yorkshire terrier. All vets will tell you that they get to know their clients well, especially in bad times when many people come to regard them as a friend in whom they can confide. It's an aspect of the job that many vets enjoy, myself included, although a major disadvantage of working at the Harmsworth is that we are often too busy to chat. Mrs Edwards brought her dog to me shortly after her husband had died. Straight away I could sense her worry and grief. Beth was obviously very ill. At twelve she was not particularly old for a Yorkie, but I discovered quickly that she had a severe infection in the womb (pyometra, from the Greek, meaning pus in the womb). Her symptoms were typical: for several days she had refused food, she had been drinking far more than usual and had started to vomit. She was dehydrated and very depressed. She looked as though she was dying and her owner was expecting the worst – I could tell that from her expression. Pyometra is one of the most common diseases that we see and hardly a day goes by without one 'pyo', as we call them, turning up in the operating theatre – and sometimes, usually on Friday afternoons, of course, two or three. Surgery to remove the ovaries and womb is the only effective treatment and it can be pretty risky: these cases may also have toxaemia, a form of blood poisoning, and may die under the anaesthetic or from complications such as kidney failure after the operation.

At first Mrs Edwards couldn't take in what I was saying: she had been expecting me to tell her that Beth should be put to sleep. But we always try to save pyos, and as many of them do very well I said I would like to try. I explained that first Beth would need a drip as she was so dehydrated from the vomiting, then I would run blood tests to check her liver and kidney function, and finally I would operate later that day. I couldn't wait more than a few hours because the infection was so severe that otherwise we might lose her. Mrs Edwards signed the consent forms and I took Beth into the hospital. I knew Mrs Edwards had some very anxious hours ahead of her and I felt for her, but there was nothing more I could do except get on with the job and keep her informed.

Beth wasn't filmed but a similar case involving another little dog was. You might think it would be difficult to talk about sensitive things in front of the cameras, and that people who were upset, perhaps tearful, would find it awkward to be filmed. In fact, once I begin a consultation I put the cameras out of my mind and concentrate on the owner and the pet. I learned quickly to forget about the other people in the room and I am sure that many owners do too.

Fortunately, with three cameras filming – one on the vet, another on the pet and owner and the third activated by remote control – we don't often need to repeat procedures. This makes for a fairly natural and calm consultation with no distress to the animal – 'fly on the wall' filming. The only artificial bit occurs when the animal has gone. The vet is sometimes asked to nod, as if they were looking at a non-existent owner, or pretend to be examining an animal by looking down at the table. These are called cutaways and may be added to the final film to give a more natural feel to questions and answers. I found the filming of cutaways rather strange at first but after a while we all got used to it. Now my standard question at the end of any filming and before I rush off for a cup of tea is, 'Any cutaways?'

While Beth was on the drip before her operation we had some encouraging news. The blood test results indicated that the kidney and liver function were normal – if pyo cases have been going on too long it is common for the kidneys and the liver to fail. Beth had a massive white cell count but this resulted from the severe infection and the body's attempt to get rid of it and I had expected it. In fact in doubtful cases we use the white cell count as a marker for the diagnosis as it is always high in pyometra.

In the afternoon we took Beth down to the operating theatre. Within the hour I had removed the septic womb and ovaries, a full ovario-hysterectomy, which is standard. The operation was a success, but that was only the first stage, and Beth was returned to the nurses, who would look after her for the next critical twenty-four hours. She would need constant monitoring and fluids, but if we could get her through this period she would stand a good chance of recovery. Yorkshire terriers are tough little dogs: a lot of people think they are lap dogs but they like to be outdoors in all weathers, like any other dog.

The next day on my ward rounds Beth was barking at me and had already decided which nurse was her favourite. She was on her feet, had managed to totter to the dog run on her own, and had not suffered any post-operative vomiting. I was delighted – and even more so when, after another twenty-four hours of care, Beth had showed an amazing improvement. It was obvious that she would be better off at home. Later that day there was a tearful reunion with her owner: Beth was jumping up and dancing around in tight circles and the nurse had to grab her to calm her down – just in case she popped one of her stitches. Dogs and cats usually do better when they are nursed at home, especially if their owner is dedicated. Home comforts, constant attention and favourite food accelerate the healing process.

Ten days later I removed Beth's stitches. She had taken on a new lease of life, was lively and full of zest. Animals' powers of recuperation are astonishing. Of course it's the devoted owner who makes the difference, and it was lovely to see Beth trotting out of the hospital with Mrs Edwards, both looking a lot happier than they had ten days ago. I hoped it was the start of better times for them both.

Removing the womb and ovaries of a seriously sick

dog is high-risk surgery, and from time to time we lose the patient, which is always sad. Prevention, though, is better than cure and unless you plan to breed your pet, it makes sense to have your female – and males too, for that matter – neutered, which can be done when they reach the age of around six months. When it is performed on fit, young, healthy animals, the operation carries the lowest of risks and is any vet's most routine operation. It holds considerable advantages for both the pet and its owner. First, the animal no longer comes into season and therefore does not attract the attention of all the male animals from miles around. Second, there are no unwanted puppies or kittens. Third, diseases of the womb, such as pyometra, cannot occur and the operation also protects against the development of breast cancer later in the animal's life.

Most people love their pets and do their best when they are ill. The degree of care can vary a lot, however, from dedicated owners like Beth's to others who seem unmoved by their animal's plight. I never did find out what Mr Gilroy called his dog and he showed little interest in her apart from bringing her to us when the symptoms started. At first these were difficult to pinpoint. She had difficulty in eating, particularly swallowing, and was stiff when she walked. She was a large lurcher-type dog – a breed we often see at the hospital. Lurchers make lovely pets, which is not always appreciated by animal lovers, and they are always difficult to rehome. Perhaps their size is off-putting.

Mr Gilroy's dog had the usual loving temperament

of a lurcher but didn't seem keen on her owner and she seemed a bit depressed. He was worried about her stiffness but I couldn't find any obvious problem with her legs, apart from a small septic wound in one. I sent her home with some antibiotics, expecting her to recover within a few days. She came back much worse: her legs seemed to have seized up and she had stopped eating.

I admitted her for further investigation and the next day, as I was passing her kennel, I saw her trying to drink. Her head went into a horrible spasm, which caused her ears nearly to meet in the centre. I tried to open her mouth but it was locked shut. So that was it: tetanus – or, as it is often called, lockjaw. It's a disease you expect to find in horses but it was only the second time I had seen it in a dog. It is caused by a germ called *Clostridium tetani*, which gets into contaminated wounds where it grows and produces the tetanus toxin, which is responsible for the symptoms. My only other case had died after a week of intensive treatment, and I it had taken me a while to get over it. I knew now that we had a real battle on our hands, which would be either won or lost by the nurses. I got some antitoxin from the local general hospital and cursed myself for not thinking of tetanus earlier – we had lost a couple of vital days.

The dog's spasms became much more frequent and her ears were permanently cocked at an angle of forty-five degrees. I gave her massive doses of penicillin and constant fluids into a vein through a catheter. She couldn't stand and the nurses had to turn her every few hours to prevent the development of bed sores. Mr

Gilroy was phoning us only every few days – a warning sign that he might dump his dog – so I rang him and agreed to update him every day. I told him that we had a fight on our hands, which we might easily lose. He just grunted and said, 'Well, get on with it and do what you have to.'

The next few days were critical and I was worried about whether or not to carry on. This is always a dilemma with a disease like this, which causes such suffering. Although the animal's misery can be lessened with modern painkillers and sedatives, we can only justify allowing it to continue if we can reasonably expect a cure. For several days, I agonised, wondering whether I should put the dog to sleep. I wasn't helped by the apparent lack of interest or commitment from her owner when I voiced my doubts to him as to whether we should continue with the treatment, he said, not very helpfully, that he would leave the decision to me.

However, the nurses were determined to get her better and by the eighth day we could see, perhaps, the beginning of an improvement in her condition. The terrible spasms in her mouth had stopped and we could open it just wide enough to get liquids into her. She could now stand with a little support and her nurse was giving her physiotherapy, gently manipulating her legs to keep the joints from stiffening up and massaging her muscles. After while we could stop the sedation and further encouraging signs began to appear. First she could take a few steps, looking rather like a rocking horse, and then she tried to wag her tail. Gradually she could open her mouth properly and she started to eat her own food.

After three weeks of tremendously hard work we could see that she would make a full recovery – but what a fight it had been. In the end it had come down to a personal battle, which everyone had wanted to see through. Mr Gilroy was subdued when he came in to take his dog home, but she seemed pleased to see him. She licked him and wagged her tail – a more demonstrative response than when she was first ill. I was surprised to see that he was crying: I had assumed that because he had been slow to phone he didn't care. I was wrong. Later he told me that every time he phoned he expected to hear the worse and couldn't bear to be in touch every day. As for visiting, he had been frightened that this would somehow be a bad omen.

We didn't need to see his dog again because she was fully recovered but one of the nurses spotted her in the park about a month later, racing around with some greyhounds, and Mr Gilroy with some friends.

I had been expecting Mr Gilroy not to pick up his dog and it was nice to be proved wrong. Sometimes, though, a pet is dumped even though it is perfectly fit, well and ready to go home. One such case was Sheba, a German shepherd, who had arrived as an extreme emergency. A ball was stuck at the entrance to her windpipe. Fortunately she hadn't been far from the hospital but she arrived fighting for breath. What could be seen of her tongue was an ominous blue colour – she wasn't getting enough oxygen into her lungs – and she was panicking understandably and difficult to control. Urgent action was required, a rapid general anaesthetic, but this would be risky. Jeremy, who had been at the hospital since he had qualified six years before, was on hand and he quickly gave Sheba an injection of anaesthetic to keep her still, then pulled out the ball from the back of her throat and gave her some oxygen. She was saved, in a matter of minutes.

Her anxious owner, a young man, was reassured that she would be all right and although Jeremy toyed with the idea of sending Sheba home he decided to keep her in for the night just to be on the safe side. The owner telephoned after midnight, sounding worried, but was told that everything had gone well, there was no cause for concern and that he could pick her up in the morning.

First thing next morning, there was Sheba, barking for her breakfast and greeting everybody with a wag, her tongue a lovely pink. The hospital was full so I told the nurse to contact the owner and say that he could pick her up right away. She was back twenty minutes later to say that the number was unobtainable and that she had checked with BT. Warning bells rang but maybe the owner would ring or come in to collect his dog.

Sadly we always have two or three animals in the hospital that are abandoned by their owners. Either they give a false address and telephone number or they don't ring after the operation. We have a set protocol for dealing with this situation: first we ring the owner, if they are on the telephone, as soon as we realise that they have not been in touch. Either the phone number is incorrect, as in Sheba's case, or we speak to the owner, who promises to pick up their pet. The next step, a few days later, is to send an ambulance driver or inspector to their home to request that they pick up the animal. Often this establishes that the address is false. Finally we send a recorded delivery letter stating that we will rehome the pet if it isn't collected within seven days.

All this was done in Sheba's case but to no avail. A week later when we had heard nothing from the owner I was faced with the problem of where to send her. She couldn't stay indefinitely at the Harmsworth. Luckily, her story caught the eye of one of the BBC researchers and she was featured briefly in one of the programmes. As usual the switchboard collapsed under the strain of tens of thousands of calls from people who wanted Sheba. It is at times like this that we know the British really are a nation of animal lovers. A veterinary surgeon with a nearby practice got in first, faxing my office at seven in the morning, and a week later Sheba was settling into her new home on the outskirts of London with another German shepherd as her playmate.

And her original owner? Well, he had been seen out and about by his neighbours but he ignored all our attempts to get in touch. Innumerable knocks on the door, cards left asking him to phone us and, of course, the recorded delivery letter had no effect. If only owners like him would just tell us that they would like their pet rehomed. It would make life a lot easier!

When I've seen all the dogs, I go on to the cats. Ward three is the first of these. We usually have many more cats than dogs – often up to sixty cats at a time of which half will be healthy strays. The reports nurse spends part of her day phoning all the homing centres within a radius of a hundred miles to see if they will take them in. Like ward three, ward four contains owned cats. I can instantly tell which is which. The owned cats have large yellow cards on which all their clinical information is recorded, which remain in the filing system for a few years. The strays are shipped out to homing centres as soon as possible and have white ward cards, stored separately.

Familiarity breeds contempt and it's easy as a vet to be caught out with a problem that seems at first to be routine. In the spring we see many cat-bite abscesses as the toms fight over the females, and on first examination this was what we thought had happened to Coco, a Siamese and very beautiful. Cats have expressive eyes and it is never hard to work out how they are feeling. I could easily see that Coco was very unhappy. There was a small wound on his chest, oozing blood and pus, which was sore to touch. I clipped it up and started to reach for the antibiotic injection. But something wasn't quite right. For a start, Coco was far too dull for a simple cat-bite abscess. I took his temperature. It didn't even register on the thermometer, a really bad sign. I looked at his tongue: it was pale and sickly in colour, instead of the salmon-pink of the healthy cat.

Coco's owner soon picked up my anxiety. Mrs Cook was a widow and Coco was her last link with her husband. The two had been inseparable and Coco hadn't eaten properly for a month after Mr Cook had died a year before. 'He's not going to die, is he?' she asked. I replied that I wasn't sure yet what was wrong.

I looked at the wound again. Surely it wasn't a cat-bite abscess. The hole was too round and neat. Suddenly, I had a horrible thought: air-gun pellet. 'I'm going to take an X-ray,' I told Mrs Cook. 'I'm afraid Coco might be very ill and I want to make sure he hasn't been shot.'

First I put Coco on a fluid drip, in case I needed to do a long operation: he would need the fluids to counteract the shock, which often occurs with heavy blood loss after operations, road accidents or severe wounds. The circulation is shunted to spare the major organs, the heart and brain particularly, and the skin becomes pale and cold. If the shock is severe, the animal may die and to prevent this it is important to set up fluid replacement into a vein as soon as possible. Next I gave Coco a painkilling injection and a sedative. Within five minutes he had been x-rayed, and a little later my worst fears were confirmed. There, in the middle of Coco's abdomen, was an air-gun pellet. It had passed through his chest, through the diaphragm – the muscle that separates the chest from the abdomen – and from there into the abdomen. I telephoned Mrs Cook and asked her how long ago this might have happened. 'Well, he hasn't been himself for a few days, since Saturday night,' she replied. It was now Tuesday afternoon. If the pellet had penetrated his intestines, Coco would die from peritonitis, inflammation of the lining of the abdomen if I didn't operate right away. Even so his chances were slim.

I gave him the lightest of anaesthetics and Liz the nurse prepared him for surgery. Meanwhile I was scrubbing up and putting on sterile gloves. It didn't take long to get into Coco's abdomen and locate the pellet, which was easily removed. But then the long and painstaking work began: there were six separate holes in the intestine and I had also to repair the one in the diaphragm. Coco's abdomen contained quite a lot of pus, which I removed with a suction machine we had bought only the previous day. Two hours later I was stitching him up. Everything possible had been done. Now it was up to Coco.

While her cat was still unconscious Mrs Cook came round to see him and took away the pellet for the police to look at. It would be difficult to find the culprit but at least news would get round the neighbourhood and perhaps whoever had been responsible would be too frightened to do it again.

For the next few days the nurses checked Coco every hour. The main problem at this stage was surgical shock and his general weakness. A few days later this was replaced by the possibility that he might die from overwhelming infection and peritonitis, inflammation of the lining of the abdomen. A week later he was still very poorly, on constant fluids administered through the vein in his front leg. Even his visits from Mrs Cook didn't perk him up.

Meanwhile, of course, he was losing weight and I had to do a second, minor, operation to place a small, flexible tube through his nose and into the stomach so that the nurses could feed him liquidised food. These naso-gastric tubes are relatively new yet they are simple to put in. We use the technique all the time, and I am sure it has speeded up the recovery of countless patients. When my first daughter was born prematurely she was fed by tube in the same way so I have the unusual experience of having done it myself in babies and cats! We kept this up for a further week, giving Coco twice daily doses of cephalexin, the most potent antibiotic we have for this kind of case.

At last, after two weeks in the hospital, he suddenly turned the corner. He started to lap on his own, in spite of the naso-gastric tube, which we removed. Once cats start to improve they don't look back, and within three days Coco was definitely interested in food. Time to go home. His owner came to pick him up and this time he was pleased to see her. Within a week he was back to normal, and even though he had been shot, he hated being kept inside at home so much that Mrs Cook had to let him out.

Air guns are so destructive that I have always felt that they should be restricted like any other firearm. I have seen hundreds of air-gun wounds in animals but never one with quite such devastating effects as Coco's.

From ward four I go to ward seven. Wards five and six house isolation cases, such as cats with serious flu or dogs with parvo virus, and I always go there last. In ward seven there may be up to thirty stray cats. Distressingly, most are lovely animals who seem to be owned, but less than ten per cent are claimed. The best way to identify a cat or a dog is to have a microchip implanted under its skin. This contains a number which is kept on a central database with all the owner's details. It is a simple matter to pass a portable scanner over the animal and, with a bleep, the number appears on the screen. Within hours animal and owner are reunited. Finding a chip is rare, though, and cats especially are unidentified. Barrels and discs fall off collars and sometimes the whole collar is lost.

While I'm in ward seven I often find myself reflecting on the problems of identifying pets as I try to work out what to do with the twenty cats in front of me. Usually half have injuries of varying severity, mostly following road accidents. The rest are fit and ready to rehome, but the report nurse often has to tell me that she can find only three or four spaces at the rehoming centres. In other words, we have too many cats for too few owners. The nurse also phones round police stations, local veterinary clinics and the regional RSPCA office to find out if any cats have been reported missing, but after all this effort few cats are reunited with their owners, which makes me think that many have been abandoned. Thousands were dumped in the summer of 1996, especially in August, the traditional holiday month. The other time when we expect large numbers of strays is immediately after Christmas. If you are thinking of getting a pet, visit an RSPCA animal homing centre and give a good home to an animal that will have been vaccinated, neutered and micro-chipped. Although kittens are appealing, adult cats almost invariably settle into a new home with relish and they are usually house-trained too.

One cat who fell victim to a confused identity was a female six-month-old ginger kitten. We were easily able to establish her age because her permanent teeth, which would have erupted at five months, had come through fully. She was very affectionate and even though she was hurt she purred and rubbed herself frantically against the nurses and anyone else who happened by.

She was scanned for the microchip – negative, worse luck. But *surely* she was owned. Although she was not suffering from shock, one of her legs was broken. She could not use it at all and spent most of her time with it held up, trying not to move, unless someone came by in which case she would struggle to her feet and walk on three legs. I examined her carefully and soon found the tell-tale sign of a traffic accident. All four paws had scuffed claws: when a cat is hit it digs its claws into the road to brake as it is bowled along.

I turned my attention to the leg. This appeared to be broken at the bottom of the femur – the thigh bone – and if this was so it would almost certainly be at the level of the growing cartilage near the knee joint. This is a supracondylar fracture and we often see it in cats of this age. However, we had to take an X-ray to confirm the diagnosis. This was scheduled for the next day and in the meantime Ginger, as we called her, was soon tucking into a specially prepared meal of chopped-up chicken, purring furiously as she ate. She had already become a favourite with the nurses – they had drawn a couple of little hearts beside her name 'Str. N19'. That was all we knew about her, that she had been picked up in London N19.

The next day Stan X-rayed her. Originally from Barbados, he qualified as a vet at Liverpool University and has been at the Harmsworth for seven years. Ginger had to have a general anaesthetic first because the knee, or stifle joint as we call it, is awkward to X-ray if the animal won't keep perfectly still. The X-ray confirmed the diagnosis that she indeed had a supracondylar fracture of the leg. Stan called me off ward rounds to have a look. For once the list wasn't too busy and he wanted to know whether he should go right ahead and fix it. This is not an easy decision to make because if no owner appeared it would be difficult to home the kitten and if anything went wrong I might be faced then with the prospect of having to put her to sleep. While we pondered she was blissfully asleep.

'Well she does look very much owned, and she's only been in two days,' I said. 'Might as well go ahead.' And I left Stan to it.

As a young vet working at the Harmsworth I had investigated four different ways of fixing supracondylar fractures. You could put in either a steel pin, or two 'rush pins', or one screw, or a three-hole plate. Now, twenty-five years later, none of those four methods is used! I expected Stan to repair the fracture with two small wires called Kirschner wires (K-wires for short) which is not too difficult when you have done, as Stan has, dozens of such operations.

Sure enough, on ward rounds the next day there was Str. N19 trying to sit up and tucking into more chicken. The X-rays – before and after the operation – were attached to her cage and looked satisfactory. So far so good. I put up Ginger for a full vaccination – it would be a shame to get this far and then have her go down with a preventable illness. Meanwhile Jill, the reports nurse, made a note to phone round all the vets in the N19 area to see if a female ginger kitten had been reported missing. The next day she told me that she had had no joy. But it was still relatively early – only four days since the kitten had arrived and she was making a good recovery. She was on twice daily painkilling injections, which is routine for our post-operative orthopaedic cases, and seemed in little discomfort. A day later I stopped the injections altogether.

But ward seven was filling up fast and we had gone over the twenty mark, which is always bad as it is so difficult to get them all out. Too many cats on the ward increases the risk of infection – a long-stayer might develop flu or, at best, mild sneezing from a newcomer which would then need treatment in isolation and diminish their chances of successful rehoming. The centres do not want to risk contaminating their residents.

For the rest of the day I found myself thinking about the ginger kitten. The report nurse said she would phone round all the local vets again and double check on our computer database of lost pets. About half an hour later she phoned me and said a male ginger kitten had been reported missing by a Mrs Blake a few days after the one in ward seven had been admitted. It was from the same area and the owner had phoned to see if there were any male ginger kittens in the hospital. She had been told that we only had females except for a couple of tabbies. We both had the same thought: could the owner have been mistaken? We checked the A to Z. Stray N19 had been picked up a couple of streets away from where the male kitten lived. On the phone Mrs Blake was doubtful – she had been assured by the pet shop that her kitten was male and she didn't want to raise the hopes of her four-year-old, who hadn't slept properly since his pet went missing. With a little gentle persuasion she agreed to come in with her little boy.

A few hours later they were being ushered into ward seven by Jill. To our amazement and delight they instantly recognised 'Ginger'. The little kitten leapt to her feet and everyone could hear the purrs from six feet away. There was no doubt that she had found her owners, who told me of how she had gone missing. They had had her since she was about six weeks old when she'd been brought to the pet shop because her mother had stopped feeding her and she seemed to be fending well enough for herself. Four-year-old Ben had fallen in love with her and Mrs Blake had bought the kitten for ten pounds, which she couldn't really afford as she was a single parent. She was saving up for the vaccinations and neutering operation but hadn't yet seen a vet, who, of course, would have put her straight as far as the kitten's sex was concerned. Ginger had not been allowed out as she hadn't been vaccinated, and had led a quiet life. She hadn't been prepared for her first sight of a dog. One of Ben's friends had come round with his parents and they had brought the family dog, a friendly Jack Russell who apparently loved cats. But as soon as she saw the dog Ginger had shot out of the open front door and disappeared. Seeing the family reunited with their pet made my day. They came back three weeks later for me to check her progress. I X-rayed the leg, which had healed completely, gave her the second vaccination and spayed her. Now if a stray cat fits the description and was found in the right area I always disregard the sex. It can be a little difficult in young kittens for the owner to work it out!

We had a similar story recently, involving another stray cat. This one had severe injuries: an eye had to be removed and a broken jaw repaired. After a week of intensive nursing, with naso-gastric feeding and painkillers, we were having no luck in finding the cat's owners. Meanwhile, unknown to us, the owners had found another cat so severely injured in the road nearby that they could not be sure if it was theirs, but had taken it to their local vet. In the event, after a tough battle, the cat died, and the owners were devastated.

As our stray cat began to improve one of the nurses spent her lunch hour ringing round the local vets to see if a similar cat had been reported missing. (We had not heard of one but a call to the local vet sometimes yields a result although you have to be persistent: there may have been a delay in the cat being reported missing) Eventually the nurse found a possible match and the incredulous owners came in. After all the anguish they had suffered in losing their pet, they were suddenly and unexpectedly reunited. It was a happy ending and the nurse who had worked so hard towards it found her reward in the delight of the owners when they identified their cat and took it home.

But stories like this are rare and, depressingly, stray cats are hardly ever claimed. If your cat goes missing don't forget to phone the RSPCA to find out if it has been handed in, and to have your pet's details registered on the computer: each regional office enters missing animals onto a database so that information can be accessed quickly. And *don't* get a kitten unless you are committed to lifelong care, which includes vaccinating, microchipping and, very importantly, neutering it.

Occasionally we are reminded that even careful owners can be caught out. When we are filming the television programme, every Wednesday morning is dedicated to making the links between the various items. This was mainly Rolf's job and it was often done in a ward using a cage as background. On one such occasion a cute cat was selected to be in the background and the actual shot took probably no more than ten or twenty seconds. But that was long enough for her owner to recognise her. She had been missing for more than a month, but the really amazing thing was that she lived on the south coast. Apparently this cat was fascinated by cars and would hop into one if the door was left open. The owners can only surmise that this was what had happened and that somehow she had found her way to London. She had been wearing a collar and disc but this had been lost. Needless to say, when cat and owner were reunited the first thing they did was to get the cat microchipped. This cat was lucky, or rather her owner was. It is not unknown for cats to attempt the long trek home and some cats have even made it, months later, but many are permanently lost or, worse, run over.

CHAPTER TWO

Something Exotic

The last stop on the rounds is ward eight, the exotic ward. To small-animal vets anything that's not a dog or cat gets lumped under the general term 'exotic', and that includes common pets like hamsters, mice, rabbits or guinea pigs as well as parrots, cockatiels, wild birds and animals, and reptiles. We don't have specialist skills to deal with many of these animals so my main aim is to decide where best to send them within twenty-four to forty-eight hours.

'Exotic' means from abroad or foreign, and I was

amused to discover in the *Oxford English Dictionary* that in 1629 'foreign' meant outlandish or barbarous. Not all the exotic pets that come to us are foreign but some are certainly outlandish, never mind barbarous. It is quite extraordinary what some people keep as a pet. Perhaps I'm old-fashioned, but to me the word pet conjures up a dog or cat – not a tarantula or a poisonous snake. Those are definitely for the hobbyist or dedicated enthusiast – perhaps a member of a club or professional organisation.

Before you buy an 'exotic' pet it is vitally important that you find out as much about the animal as possible, especially the specialised care it will need. Most problems and diseases encountered by vets are due to the owner's failure to provide a proper environment and/or feeding for their the animal. At present, there is no legislation to deter potential owners so we do the best we can, but often we have to tell them that they must take their pet to a vet with specialist knowledge of that particular species – which, of course, is expensive. Nevertheless, ward eight is often full to overflowing.

One Monday morning I found myself examining an animal I hadn't treated before, a chinchilla called Henry. The chinchilla is a South American rodent, related to the guinea pig. In the wild, they live high up in the Andes at an altitude of 4,500 metres and it is a tribute to the species that they have adapted to our climate. They have been bred in captivity since the 1920s but they are still hardy enough to survive at as low a temperature as freezing point, if they are kept in dry conditions. The ideal temperature, though, is around 10–20°C. A curious feature of the animal in captivity is that in order to keep its fur clean, it needs a daily bath in volcanic dust!

I had been told to handle chinchillas with care, not because they bite, which they virtually never do – but because if they are handled roughly the fur can slip away from the body – 'fur slip' – which takes a long time to heal. Henry was five, middle-aged for a chinchilla and had been admitted to the ward for two reasons – both potentially serious. First, he had been having a little trouble eating and was salivating, which had caused the fur around his mouth to become moist, leaving the area open to infection. Second, he had passed a little blood in his urine. On the previous Friday he had been given an anaesthetic, not a light undertaking as small animals like chinchillas are fragile and you have to be careful not to give them too much. He was put into a transparent plastic chamber into which gas was passed, and when he was unconscious he was transferred to a mask, which fitted neatly over his snout. When he was deeply asleep, the mask was removed and we looked at his teeth. They were overgrown – especially the molars – and we trimmed them back. At the same time we X-rayed his bladder to see if there were any bladder stones and took a urine sample. Ten minutes later we let him come round.

We didn't find any bladder stones but there was protein and blood in the urine sample. This suggested cystitis, or inflammation of the bladder. Over the weekend, he was given antibiotic injections and we wanted to see if he could eat. His owner had brought in special chinchilla pellets but we also offered him fresh hay and a little dry fruit and nuts. When I next saw him I picked him up gently and looked at his mouth. The skin around it was dry – an obvious improvement – and the chart on his cage demonstrated his eating, drinking and ablutions were also improving. He could go home. In the short term he had a good prognosis and he was fortunate in having good owners – a family with two children who had read everything ever written on chinchillas (which isn't much) – but in the long term his teeth would continue to cause problems. I expected to see him again at some point, but I suggested to the owners that they get a block of wood for him to gnaw on which might help to wear down his teeth. They would have to give him antibiotics as a syrup by mouth for the next ten days and then we would check his urine again. Happily, he made a good recovery.

In a cage opposite Henry was Ziggy, a young iguana. When I qualified I never dreamed of treating an animal like this and it is only in the last few years that significant numbers have started to appear. They do not make ideal pets as within about five years they can grow up to six feet in length, and become dangerous and difficult to handle. Many are bought as a status symbol and in a few years' time we may see widespread abandonment of them. In their native Central/South America they are mainly tree-dwelling and found in tropical forests. It is hard to imagine a more different environment from a London flat. In the wild, iguanas are vegetarian and live on flowers, fruit and vegetables. They need to be kept in large enclosures, which are sufficiently high that branches can be provided for climbing, in a warm, moist atmosphere, up to 35°C during the day and 25°C at night, with 60–90% humidity. Specialised heat lamps and lighting are needed so that the animal can bask as it would in its natural environment.

If this were not enough to put off all but the most knowledgeable enthusiast, feeding is not straightforward either. Although iguanas are vegetarian, the correct balance of food still has to be maintained to include plant matter, high-protein matter and fruit. Experts also recommend supplementing the diet of juveniles with vitamins and minerals.

Ziggy was small, only about nine inches long, and had already suffered from his owner's ignorance. He had been bought from a pet shop because the owner had 'liked the look of him'. He had come into ward eight because the owner suspected his legs were broken and he was apparently not eating. Both Ziggy's forelimbs and one of his hindlimbs were swollen and he was having difficulty moving about. He was also rather thin. Stan X-rayed him and confirmed that all three legs were broken: Ziggy's bones contained very low levels of calcium due to inadequate supplementation and they had become so brittle that the merest act of moving was enough to break them. On the X-ray the outer part of the bones, the cortices, were hardly visible: in healthy animals the cortices can be seen normally as a sharp white line.

Things were so bad that we warned the owner that the outlook for Ziggy was grim. We gave him calcium injections and in the first few days we had to try to telephoning and poor Ziggy was showing no sign of response to treatment. In fact, he went gradually downhill and in spite of our efforts he died. A few days later the nurse in charge of the exotics ward managed to get hold of his owner, who seemed neither concerned nor upset.

Until restrictions are placed on the purchase of animals like Ziggy, many others will suffer the same fate. As Ziggy had been admitted as an emergency I hadn't met his owner and I was keen to talk to him and find out why he had bought the iguana – and to get some idea as to why he had lost interest so quickly. I wanted to get some insight into how these pets are marketed, so that perhaps we could develop a strategy to discourage the impulse-buying of them. I sent a note to Ziggy's owner asking him to come and see me, but it was ignored. With any luck iguanas will soon go out of fashion and suffering like Ziggy's will be prevented.

Ziggy's owner might not have been too bothered about his pet, but the owners of the little juvenile terrapin were devastated when they found out that they had caused near blindness in their pet through incorrect feeding. The terrapin had come in with his eyes so puffed up that he couldn't see, and he'd been fed on mince and fish fillets, neither of which were suitable, and was suffering from a lack of vitamin A – a problem familiar to most vets. Also his tank water was dirty with rotting food, a breeding ground for infection, although at first sight I couldn't find any evidence of this. Several things had to be done. First, the terrapin – his owners hadn't got round to giving him a name – was admitted for treatment and observation. Second, he had to be tempted with the right feed, which the owners would be taught to give him in a separate feeding area and we made up a diet sheet based on the recommendations in the *BSAVA Manual of Exotic Pets*, an excellent book on which we rely heavily, and included fish, prawns, shrimps, cubes of cheese and terrapin pellets. He would also receive a special terrapin supplement of minerals and vitamins. The third and most important part of his treatment was vitamin A injections, given weekly for four weeks or more. Once we had persuaded him to start eating his outlook was good, and the children of the family were itching to get him home.

A lot of terrapins were bought during the craze for Ninja turtles and few people realised how badly things could go wrong if they didn't look after their pet correctly. However, good feeding and management bring their own problems: these animals can grow into the size of dinner plates, whereupon they need a huge tank and lose their appeal. When they are abandoned, it is often very difficult to rehome them.

If some exotic pets are abandoned by their owners many are lost, and we encounter huge numbers of domestic rabbits. They are found hopping up main roads, in people's gardens, in telephone kiosks, you name it – and they are virtually never reclaimed. They are extraordinarily difficult to rehome too. We have had as many as twenty all at once, and have tried desperately hard to place them. The alternative, hated by all of us, is to put them to sleep. This is, of course, the definite last resort, and somehow we have usually been able to avoid it, but it sometimes means that they have to stay for a month or so, tying up a nurse who has to attend to them.

Things came to a head on the rabbit front one week during the filming of *Animal Hospital* – I had so many in I had hardly any room left in the exotics ward for any other animals. I had a chat with one of the producers to see if we could feature their plight. The problem, of course, is not confined to the Harmsworth: all the homing centres are full to capacity with them. It appears that when a rabbit goes missing few people bother to look for them. Perhaps they think that a rabbit will come in, like a cat, when hungry. Not so. A rabbit left unrestrained will simply wander off. Young or small rabbits are often eaten by the innumerable urban foxes but the bigger ones usually end up with us.

The camera crew graphically portrayed our dilemma: they filmed one of the nurses looking after some rabbits and another crew went up to our homing centre at Southridge kennels near Potters Bar. There, they could see for themselves the extent of the problem: fifty-eight rabbits were waiting for new homes and some would have to be put down to make way for new arrivals. The longest-stay residents would be the first to go.

When the programme went out there was another explosion on the switchboard. The next day at Southridge, cars began to arrive at 8 a.m. and by ten there was a queue several hundred yards' long. In twenty-four hours we had rehomed the entire stray rabbit collection of the RSPCA. Some of the new homes were the last word in luxury: specially designed rabbit hutches with all rabbit mod-cons. But, sadly, a year later we were back to the same situation: every week three or more were waiting for new homes.

Rabbits need special care and attention or, given the opportunity, they will wander off. My inspector friends tell me they see many cases of cruelty every year simply because people forget about their rabbits and leave them in hutches without food. They can suffer terribly in winter when the long, cold nights and short days mean that children, so often the nominal owners, don't venture out to care for them. Yet some people have found that rabbits, with very little training, make good in-house pets: they can be taught to use a litter tray, make little mess around the house and lead infinitely more comfortable lives than their unfortunate friends banished outside to solitary confinement. Rabbits deserve a break.

Yet another animal that as a newly qualified vet I never saw myself treating is the rat. As far as my formal training was concerned, it didn't exist. Recently, though, there has been a steady increase in the number kept as pets and it is easy to see why. Fancy rats are charming, friendly little animals and they make excellent children's pets, although many people shudder at the thought of them, perhaps because of the less than wholesome reputation of their wild cousins, who even now are responsible for spreading diseases. Pet rats are easy to feed as commercial pellets are available. Curiously, they like chocolate and cakes – which should only be fed in small quantities – and we used this arcane piece of rat lore to encourage Jason to eat during treatment for his illness.

He had come into the clinic as he was off colour and not eating. His owner, Jane, was very attached to him and had owned him for two years which is about half his expected life span. When she arrived I asked, 'Where's the animal?' As if on cue a little head popped up from within her jacket and sniffed the air cautiously. Then, not liking what he sensed, he popped back out of sight. Jane thrust her hand down her front and, after some fun and games, managed to fish him out. After that he submitted passively to my examination. (That's another thing I like about rats: they are usually docile and rarely bite.) An examination didn't reveal much, but when I palpated Jason's tummy he let of a small quantity of urine on the table. I made the most of the opportunity and tested it with a paper stick, which gives a surprisingly large amount of information in just one minute. Jason's urine contained some protein but a lot of blood, which suggested that he had a bladder infection. At least I had something to go on. I jabbed him with some antibiotic and sent him home with some antibiotic syrup that is designed for children, but is useful for treating rats and other exotics too.

A week later Jason hadn't made any progress – if anything he was a little worse and wasn't eating at all. There was only one thing for it – we would have to admit him for tests to see if we could get a diagnosis. Keeping animals under observation is useful as sometimes we can see for ourselves quite clearly what the problem is. Jason did little over the first few days except refuse food and lie about. One morning he seemed to be breathing a little faster and I decided to take an X-ray of his chest. With a wriggly rat this is by no means easy and in the end I had to give him just a little gas to keep him still on the X-ray plate for a few seconds while we took a picture.

Checking through various articles and books, I found out that rats are susceptible to lung infections and that they often have severe infections without showing much in the way of symptoms. Could this be Jason's problem? Again an X-ray would be the best way to find out. As the film came rolling out of our automatic processor, a gift from the Friends of the Harmsworth, I was pleased to see at once that it was well exposed and should tell us what we needed to know. Sure enough, Jason's lungs were very congested and I couldn't see the outline of his heart at all clearly. It looked as though he had a severe lung infection which had produced some fluid – possibly pus – that was gradually filling up his chest. This would explain his breathing problem. It was worrying that he hadn't responded to the antibiotic syrup, and I discussed our next options with Jane, who was tearful at the prospect of losing him. According to the texts, these cases are difficult to cure but it can be done. We decided to try him with cephalexin, which had saved Coco, the cat which had been shot. This would be given daily by the nurses. Meanwhile we would tempt him to eat with his favourite chocolate and cake. For a few days nothing happened. Then, suddenly, he took a piece of chocolate, some pellets, and perked up.

Back on my ward round, I held him while I listened to his chest and tried to decide whether or not to send him home. Stress is a potent cause of disease in both humans and animals, there are few things more stressful than being in hospital. On balance it was probably better for him to be at home. I borrowed some cephalexin drops from a vet friend up the road and asked Jane to take over the treatment at home with a dropper. She called in later for Jason's nurse to show her how to get the drops into his mouth with the minimum of fuss. When we last heard of him, he was doing well.

Jane would have to be careful in the long term, though, because once a small animal's lungs are damaged, they are prone to recurrences of infection – a bit like the lungs of chronic smokers. I always advise owners with animals who have lung complaints not to smoke near them – there is plenty of evidence that a smoky atmosphere can cause disease in animals or make existing lung disease worse. In this respect animals are no different from us: they need a good, healthy environment to live in and clean air to breathe, and this is particularly true of the exotic and small animals who don't have very big lungs.

Ward eight is where we locate wild animals, those who live in close proximity to people and are welcomed and looked upon as friends. For many weeks of the year we have several hedgehogs under treatment. Probably their only enemies in London are dogs, foxes and motor cars, and these little animals are universally regarded as the gardener's friend. Their natural diet consists of slugs, snails, earthworms, insects, some fruit and whatever people put out for them.

We see them with a fairly wide variety of complaints, from injuries caused by dog attacks and road accidents to medical problems. Examining a hedgehog is far from easy: at the first hint of danger they roll up into a tight ball and no part of the body is accessible. There are various techniques to get them to unwind, but none is infallible. Our favourite is to stroke the back towards the tail – I use gloves to do this – and when a back leg comes into view this can be gently grabbed. It has to be said that the more street-wise hedgehogs are obstinate, and if all else fails we have to resort to anaesthesia.

Once we had three hedgehogs in together; two were suffering from a similar condition although they had not come from the same part of London. Both appeared as a result of calls from people who had found them apparently ill in their gardens. When we examined them we found they had respiratory infections, which are quite common in hedgehogs. Their breathing was quite noisy and they had the snuffles. Their treatment consisted of daily antibiotics, given by injection, multivitamins, also by injection, and plenty of good food. During the week both sets of 'owners' had phoned faithfully every day. Its heart-warming that so many people care not only about their pets but about wild animals in their gardens. I decided to keep them in for another five days – with winter coming on we would have to be very sure that the hedgehogs were fit and healthy before we released them.

Returning hedgehogs to the wild is normally done at dusk as they are nocturnal animals and it is safer for them. When we were filming the first series, a hedgehog was apparently released in daylight, for obvious reasons, although in fact he was to remain a captive until that night. That wasn't the impression the film gave, though, and I received many critical letters.

That's another lesson I've learned: be careful what you say or do on television as hundreds of people are waiting out there to pounce! Many of the letters were nice and constructive, but some didn't mince words...

The third hedgehog, Horace, had apparently been abandoned – at least that was what we were told by the member of the public who brought him in. He weighed 250 gms, which is rather small, and he was probably only seven or eight weeks old. Although he was taking solid food it was now autumn and any hedgehog weighing less than 450 gms in the wild in late autumn has little chance of surviving the winter. Thus Horace needed someone to look after him and build him up to his adult weight of 1,000 gms or so. As always, with our charges in ward eight, this involved lots of phone calls to find a foster home. Finally someone offered to take him on, and he was kept warm and fed throughout the winter, which meant he didn't need to hibernate. By the spring he was ready to be released. At dusk, on a pleasant, mild day, he was allowed to wander off in a safe, quiet garden and soon settled into his new home.

Some patients stay rather longer in ward eight and a couple to whom we willingly gave house room were Bill and Ben, two budgies who were with us for three weeks. They belonged to Mrs Davies, a seventy-five-year-old widow. I knew her quite well, because she had nursed her cat with kidney failure for eighteen months. She had rescued him, a 'retired' (neutered) old bruiser of a tabby called Bruce, eight years earlier. He had developed kidney failure slowly but by a combination of diet – low protein and low salt – and long-acting injections of anabolic steroids we had managed to keep him going. I was used to seeing her once a month, along with her son who used to make the trip up from Kent so that he could transport his mother to the hospital. Against all the odds Bruce did well for those eighteen months before he developed liver cancer. Mrs Davies was shattered by his death and vowed not to have any more pets, but after a few months her son brought her two budgies as a surprise present. He felt that another cat might be too much for her but that two budgies would be easy to look after and good company. She took to them immediately and was soon back to her usual cheery self. However, both birds seemed to have a lot of crust above the beak and round the legs. The pet-shop assistant had assured Mrs Davies's son that it wasn't anything to worry about and he had parted with his cash happy in the knowledge that the budgies would soon be cheering his mother up. He had even lined up a neighbour to look after them when he took Mrs Davies on holiday to Devon.

All went well until a few days before the holiday when both budgies took a turn for the worse. More crust was developing and on one bird it had caused a little bleeding. To make matters worse, the neighbour's husband had to go in to hospital and she didn't feel able to look after the budgies, especially as they were ill and would need trips to the vet and treatment.

It was a disconsolate Mrs Davies who faced me across the consulting-room table one busy Monday afternoon. It looked as though her much-needed and looked-forward-to holiday would have to be cancelled but, worse, without her son, how would she be able to bring the birds to us? But there was an easy answer to the problem and I told Mrs Davies that we would admit the birds for treatment. They were small and would only take up one cage. And there wasn't much doubt as to what was wrong with them: the crusts round the beak and feet pointed to the aptly named 'scaly beak' and 'scaly leg', caused by a mite called *Cnemidocoptes pilae,* which infests budgies in particular and causes this awful scaling and crustiness. I picked a few scabs off one bird, put them on a glass slide and, within seconds, I saw a mite scurrying about.

The treatment is relatively simple and involves rubbing a few drops of liquid into the crusts once a week and cleaning out the cage. Within three weeks we could expect a good response which, in fact, is what happened. I had forbidden Mrs Davies even to think about phoning while she was on holiday. She could leave the worrying to us for a change and we would phone her on her return to arrange for her to pick them up. I thought of Mrs Davies while she was away and was pleased to see that Devon was enjoying a heatwave while she was down there.

After she got back, and an hour after we called her, she and her son, both looking tanned, refreshed, and happy arrived to take Bill and Ben home to a life of luxury and constant companionship. I was sorry to see the budgies go: they were talkative and great fun to have around. Budgies are nice pets and relatively easy to treat in hospital, compared to some of the ward eight patients. Also, they·are usually hardy and fit, and with a bit of luck I wouldn't need to see Bill and Ben again.

CHAPTER THREE

Working with the RSPCA

Hospitals like the Harmsworth are rare. It costs a million pounds a year just to run the Harmsworth. London has two animal hospitals – the other is in Putney; Birmingham and Manchester have one each and there are wildlife hospitals in Cheshire, Norfolk and Somerset. The rest of the country is served by the RSPCA branches, many of which have clinics. Some are quite large and well equipped while the smaller ones are staffed by volunteers and serviced by a vet in private practice, who may visit several hours a week. If a branch doesn't have a clinic it may still be able to help financially disadvantaged people with vouchers. The service we offer is subsidised, which means that charges are made according to the owner's circumstances, and we aim only to recover our costs.

We accept as clients only those who live in a defined catchment area within striking distance of the hospital and who will supply, in confidence, details of their financial situation to the administration staff. The concept of a catchment area is difficult to get across to the public and one of the disadvantages of appearing on television is that suddenly everyone wants you to treat their animal, even though we are able to do no more and no less than most other vets. Worst of all, people sometimes turn up unannounced demanding an appointment for a second opinion on their pet, occasionally having travelled long distances. The Royal College of Veterinary Surgeons' rules are clear: if an owner wishes an animal to be seen by a vet for a second opinion, a request has to be made by the first vet who will send a letter to the second detailing all treatment given so far. Second opinions are time consuming and cannot be dealt with in a routine clinic. After the first series my heart would sink to my boots when I had to deal with three or four such cases at every clinic. Now, the nurses who answer the phone are careful to ask callers where they live before making an appointment and also to find out if they have followed the correct procedure before requesting a second opinion.

Over the years I have got to know many RSPCA inspectors and we have become friends. Theirs is a tough job, especially in London. For one thing they may be confused with the police, which can be hazardous at night in some areas. They are duty-bound to investigate cruelty cases and often a knock on the door is most unwelcome: they frequently have to take police officers with them to ensure their safety. The RSPCA and the police work closely together: while an inspector will establish the facts in a cruelty case and conduct interviews, the police may be required if entry to a property is found to be necessary.

Physical fitness, common sense, tact and sometimes a thick skin are all prerequisites for the job. Often a new inspector will be posted almost immediately to London – a baptism of fire – with the prospect of moving after a few years to quieter pastures. Some like the pace and action and stay in the city, and we are lucky to have a core of highly experienced, professional inspectors, who give excellent training to new recruits.

Cruelty cases are often shocking, even to those, like me, with many years of experience. The work can be emotionally draining for a new inspector – no amount of lectures can prepare you for the real thing. The RSPCA receives thousands of applications for each inspector training course, so those who are selected are exceptional in one way or another. Some are graduates – we have one with a degree in marine biology. Others have expertise with exotic animals. Many have spent time in the armed forces, perhaps as a marine commando, submariner, soldier or military policeman. Some have had quite ordinary jobs. I have often wondered how the headquarters training staff make their selection when they have so many to choose from.

There is nearly always an inspector in the hospital, although they are not based there, and we sometimes have to call on them to sort out a disturbance of the sort that occurs when people have had one or two too many – although with the changing of the licensing hours this has fortunately become rarer!

I do only a small amount of cruelty work now, I'm glad to say. Each case can take up to five days in court and if I took on any number of them I would never be in the hospital. It is common for a defendant not to turn up for the first scheduled court appearance, which means wasted time for everyone. If a case goes to appeal we may have to spend two days in the Crown Court. I find it interesting to go to court and see justice in operation. Being aggressively cross-examined is a challenge but, in a way, enjoyable – if the facts are clear. If there is any doubt in my own mind I will often advise an inspector that there is insufficient evidence to bring a cruelty charge. I know that any such doubt will be exploited ruthlessly by the defence. Nevertheless I am always left feeling that the system is fair: the evidence has to be watertight to secure a guilty verdict.

There was absolutely no doubt that Duchess had suffered terribly but the difficulty lay in establishing who was to blame. She arrived at the hospital one morning when I was consulting – you couldn't miss her and she immediately attracted the attention of the nurses and receptionists. Her demeanour was of abject misery; she displayed minimal interest in the prodding and probing that forms part of an investigation; there was almost no hair left on her body; her entire skin was scaling and itchy; she smelt terrible.

How could this have happened? The young man who brought the dog to the hospital said he had found her in the street and taken pity on her. She was just about recognisable as an English bull terrier and he said he had always wanted one but couldn't afford to buy one. He wasn't much help with Duchess's history, which plays an important part in the diagnosis of skin disease. I simply didn't have a clue as to how Duchess's illness started or, indeed, what was wrong with her. I had to make some quick decisions, and the most important was whether we should try to cure her or put her to sleep on humanitarian grounds. Of one thing I was reasonably sure: she wouldn't do well in hospital. She needed home cooking and pampering and a dedicated owner. Would this particular young man, whose name I now knew was Simon, fit the bill?

I had my doubts. His story didn't ring true and I wasn't impressed with his reasons for wanting her. It was as though he regarded a pedigree dog as a status symbol, which is not a very good reason for taking on the responsibility of caring for a pet. When I had completed my initial examination I decided to try for a diagnosis and cure, and go with Simon at least to start with.

'What are you going to call her?' I asked.

Without any apparent thought, he replied, 'Duchess.'

I couldn't help noticing that the dog lifted her head when she heard the name. Did she belong to him anyway? And by bringing her to us was he just trying to avoid prosecution? I knew if I could find the true owner, prosecution would follow. But whatever the cause of Duchess's condition it must have taken months of neglect for her to reach this state. The great areas of rhinoceros-like skin were typical of chronic skin diseases that have been going on for a year or so.

First things first. We had to do some tests. Duchess was admitted to the isolation ward where I took multiple skin scrapings to try to establish if she had scabies. I spent an hour poring over microscope slides, looking for the mites that causes scabies and only gave up, when I was reasonably certain that they weren't there. To be sure, though, I asked the nurses to bath Duchess in the scabies shampoo. At least it brought the scale off her and we knew she had enjoyed the bath, felt better for it almost immediately, because she tucked into her food afterwards. You could almost sense that she felt she was being cared for at last – which, of course, was exactly what was happening.

English bull terriers are generally big softies, and it didn't take long for the whole hospital to grow fond of her. She had a loving character and expressive eyes that shone at you. I was completely taken in – I thought it was just me she adored – but pretty soon it was obvious that she loved everyone. It made it all the more baffling that anyone could have let her disease get to such an advanced state, and I marvelled again at how a dog which had been so ill-treated could continue to trust in the kindness of humans.

The next day Duchess faced her first local anaesthetic as I prepared her for a skin biopsy, which involved taking slivers of her skin, which would be sent for analysis by a pathologist. I sent them off hoping for a breakthrough as we still didn't know what was the matter with her, although I had some ideas: bull terriers are prone to allergies, and neglected cases can develop secondary bacterial infections.

That night Duchess's story went out on the weekly programme but none of us was prepared for what happened immediately after transmission. We received more than a hundred phone calls in the first few hours and in all more than two hundred. Each gave the same message: Duchess had been owned by Simon's brother since she was a pup. The inspectors were asked to make an urgent investigation: by then we had discharged her from the hospital while I waited for the results of the biopsy.

The next day RSPCA inspector Jon Storey went to Simon's house, removed Duchess and brought her back to the hospital – leaving me to find a home – temporary or otherwise – for the duration of her treatment. There was a bonus, though. The inspector had lengthy interviews with Duchess's owner and a picture of the disease began to emerge. It had been going on for two years, with only intermittent trips to the vet. For the last six months Duchess had had no treatment and her deterioration had been dramatic. There was clear evidence of lack of care, which was carefully documented for the prosecution that would follow.

Meanwhile we had two strokes of luck: we found a foster home for Duchess via one of our rehoming centres, and the biopsy showed clear evidence of an allergic disease. More importantly, it revealed a secondary infection with both bacteria and yeast. The yeast surprised me. Only a few weeks before I had been to a lecture about it and could have kicked myself for not thinking of it! Immediately I started a three-pronged treatment: evening primrose oil for the allergy, a powerful antibiotic for the infection, and a drug called ketoconazole for the yeast, which was not licensed for dogs but which I knew from the lecture would be effective.

Duchess's foster family came in to meet her and introduce her to their own dog – another English bull terrier. They seemed to get along fine so we waved goodbye and the two dogs trotted off happily with the children and parents. It was a temporary arrangement, but at least it would give me breathing space while I assessed what should be done. Any dog undergoing long-term treatment, whether for a broken leg or chronic skin disease, is far better off in a loving home – no amount of specialised hospital care can match it.

That day the English bull terrier club telephoned to say that Duchess should not be rehomed with another bull terrier because they might fight. The club had already sent me loads of useful information about the breed, research programmes into skin diseases, and money to help pay for Duchess's treatment, and I knew their advice should be taken seriously. But for the time being we knew Duchess would be getting lots of loving care, although I made a note to keep an eye out for a more permanent owner if things didn't work out at the foster home.

At the first check everything seemed to be fine. The two dogs were tolerating each other, after a fashion, despite the occasional dust-up. Duchess was doing spectacularly well: the scale had fallen off, the itching had stopped and new hair was growing – she looked a different dog. We were on the right track and I prescribed another month of treatment, confident that we would see an equally dramatic improvement next time. Two days later we were in trouble. Duchess and the other dog had fallen out and Duchess had caused it some nasty wounds. The foster owners had no alternative but to call it a day so we admitted her back into the hospital.

Now we had to find her a new foster home. This time she would have to be on her own and with someone as dedicated as the previous family. The next day we had another stroke of luck (Duchess was certainly making up for her two years of misfortune!). A vet phoned me to say that a friend of his was interested in homing Duchess. She was used to English bull terriers and wanted to give a loving home to one. I asked Jon Storey to do a home check, in which he would make sure that the new owner could cope with all the potential problems associated with a neglected dog. Everything proved satisfactory so Duchess was introduced to Lisa the next day. As I saw them leave I crossed my fingers – third time lucky?

Three weeks later Duchess was bouncing with health and happiness. By now she was only on the evening primrose oil and antibiotics, and her hair was shining and growing through like spring grass. She would need lifelong care and treatment but I had every confidence we could control her condition. A year later, it is hard to believe that she has gone through so much and is so well again.

Six months after we first saw Duchess, the cruelty

case came to court. Simon's brother, wisely taking advice from his defending solicitor, pleaded guilty to causing unnecessary suffering. This was unusual, though, because the majority of people in this situation receive legal aid and elect to fight, hoping that some loophole will be found either to get them off the charge or at least to minimise the fine. Duchess's previous owner was fined heavily and banned from keeping a dog for five years. For me the ban is the most important part of any prosecution since it is the only effective way to prevent further cruelty. Neighbours have long memories and the appearance of a dog in a home banned from keeping them is sure to prompt phone calls to the RSPCA.

In a case like Duchess's, once a complaint has been made about how an animal is being kept, or the animal has been found in a poor state, and prosecution has begun, the outlook for the animal is usually quite good. They are well looked after before the case comes to court, and, assuming that their owner is banned from keeping a pet, they are rehomed afterwards. And distressing as these cases are while they are in progress, I am always cheered by the knowledge that in the end it will probably turn out for the best.

Much worse is a case in which it is clear to us that an animal is in an unsatisfactory home but it is hard to prove cruelty. For example, many dogs are kept virtually in solitary confinement with barely adequate shelter and food, and hardly any human company. These animals are used mainly to deter burglars and they are not family pets. Yet dogs are social animals and it is so sad to see the results of their confinement:

they become nervous, frightened and distrustful of all humans. Others are owned by people who have their own problems which make it almost impossible for them to care for themselves let alone a pet.

Brandy was a little mongrel puppy, perhaps about eight months old, who was admitted one night with a painful leg. The vet on duty wasn't sure if it was broken so after giving the dog some painkiller injections she admitted him for the night. The owner was no help at all – he was much the worse for wear through drinking, and was unable to tell us how long the leg had been painful. Initially he was abusive to the staff, demanding immediate attention, although he had been told that the vet was still doing a Caesarean on a cat. He was about thirty and from time to time he took a swig from a large cider bottle, bellowing at his puppy now and again. Brandy was clearly terrified of him – cringing every time his owner so much as looked at him.

Eventually Brandy was admitted, but his owner was unable to sign the admission form. The next day the puppy was seen huddled at the back of the cage, looking very miserable. The nurse on his ward gave him a cuddle but even that didn't elicit a wag. However, he was already starting to put some weight on the leg and I felt all round. No evidence of any breaks, probably just bruising. I thought he could benefit from another couple of days in hospital for some tender loving care. The nurses can usually get round even the most timid animal quickly.

The next day Brandy was a lot more cheerful. I found him tucking into breakfast under the watchful eye of Carole, his nurse. His whole demeanour and facial expression had changed and he had taken a special fancy to her, wagging his tail furiously every time she glanced at him. This is a strong characteristic of dogs that haven't been well looked after: they know when people are being kind and they respond by wanting more! Some dogs even take a fancy to me, which is extraordinary if you consider that I must be a rather threatening figure in my white coat, peering at them and pulling them about with no food gifts.

Meanwhile we had had no contact from Brandy's owner, which didn't surprise us. Brandy did not need any treatment but he was lapping up the care and attention being lavished on him by Carole, and I felt sad that we would have to give him back to an obviously unsuitable owner. We could not legally take him away unless we could prove that Brandy's owner had caused him unnecessary suffering or had ill-treated him. Maybe the puppy would turn out to be a permanent dump – I hoped so because it would be easy and satisfying to find him a new, loving home. I had a pretty shrewd idea whose that might be.

No such luck. The next day Carole was looking very upset and I soon found out why. Late the previous night Brandy's owner had turned up, drunk, and demanded his dog back. On seeing the man, Brandy had cowered and his ears had gone right back. He was picked up roughly, which made him yelp. I saw some hope in that he was scheduled to return in a week for a check-up. If he did not show up I could send an inspector to investigate. Maybe we could get the dog off the owner if things were bad in the home.

A week later I was reminded of this by a nurse (not hard to guess which one). There had been no sign of Brandy or his owner, but an RSPCA inspector happened to be in the hospital on other business and I had a word with him. Later that afternoon he called at Brandy's address and found no one at home. The neighbours remembered seeing a puppy but not for the last day or so – the owner spent most of his time in the pub. The Inspector looked through the letter-box and could see Brandy. He also saw a lot of dog mess on the floor, a big bowl of dry dog food and some water. He taped up the doors of the house and left his card, stating that the puppy must be examined at the hospital within twenty-four hours or further action would be taken. Later that night he returned. The tapes were still in place: it looked as if Brandy had been abandoned for the weekend. No doubt the owner believed that by putting down what he thought would be adequate food and water it was reasonable to leave the puppy alone. This, of course, is not the case.

First thing in the morning the Inspector went back. He hardly needed to examine the tapes – he could hear Brandy whimpering. He look through the letter-box again and saw that the water bowl had been overturned. That was it. He was straight on the phone to base, requesting the assistance of the police, and within half an hour two policemen were on the scene to help him get in to rescue the dog. Half an hour later Brandy was back in hospital under the care of his favourite nurse. This time there was no going back. A few days later the owner was interviewed and charged with abandonment. Unusually he admitted everything and said he had been on a 'bender'. Furthermore he was quite happy to sign his dog over to the RSPCA for rehoming.

Next day Brandy was with Carole's parents in the country and settled in quickly. Within a few weeks it was as though he had never experienced any unkindness and had become the naturally trusting and loving dog he wanted to be. Everyone delighted in seeing photos of him walking with his new owners in the countryside and sleeping in the most luxurious dog bed you have ever seen.

We received a few phone calls from the ex-owner, who demanded to know where the dog was. Apparently he had forgotten that he had signed him over. Some months later he was in court where a light fine was imposed on him, with court costs, but he was banned for ten years from keeping a dog. People often think that a ban is unenforceable, but experience shows that it is usually respected. The penalty for not complying with a court order could be prison and a huge fine.

Lottie's case was far more clear cut. A friendly little crossbreed dog with an incessantly wagging tail, she had been left unattended for weeks. Hers was one of the most unpleasant cases of abandonment I have ever had to deal with. Her owner was a young woman who had gone away for Christmas, supposedly leaving her two dogs in the care of a friend called Angela. In the subsequent court case she was unable to give even the most trivial details of Angela, or where she lived, except that she was from Ireland and a heroin addict. The suffering of the dogs can hardly be imagined: left alone to fend for themselves, they had no chance of getting adequate food or water.

When RSPCA inspector John Bowe was contacted by the police he broke into the flat. One of the dogs had died and the other, Lottie, had survived by eating her dead companion. The police had been alerted by the neighbours because water was dripping into the flat below and a dog could be heard barking. It was probably the leak which saved Lottie: dehydration kills more quickly than starvation. When I examined her she had lost two thirds of her body weight and was in a state of extreme emaciation. All that was left of the other dog was its skull – the only part that Lottie had been unable to finish off. This grisly piece of evidence was kept as court evidence.

The nurses had to feed Lottie very carefully – little and often – as she was so ravenous and in these cases there is a big risk of tummy upsets. But Lottie went from strength to strength and within three weeks was more like her normal self. She wagged her tail furiously whenever anybody passed her cage – even the most fleeting eye contact set her off.

Meanwhile the hunt was on for her owner. Inspector John Bowe had made a note of the names on the various letters that he found unopened in the flat – and one name appeared more than any other. Extensive enquiries began – at times like this the inspectors turn into detectives and have to be extremely patient.

After a month the net closed. The owner's parents had been located and discreet enquiries confirmed her whereabouts. She was arrested by the police and questioned at length by John Bowe. She blamed the dogs' fate entirely on her friend, but could not come up with any further evidence to back her story. In court she was discredited by the RSPCA solicitor and made a poor account of herself. It was a straightforward case, more so than most cruelty cases, and although Lottie's owner was adamant that she loved animals the facts showed that she was not capable of looking after them. Apparently she had written to the RSPCA about employment as a nurse, and this was produced in court as evidence of her commitment to animals. Many times in court I have heard the same defence, but the evidence is always damning. Once all the facts of a case have been assessed it comes down to one factor – lack of care.

Lottie's owner was found guilty at the magistrates' court but appealed. The case went to the Crown Court and the proceedings took two days. I was cross-examined by a barrister for over an hour. I was, as always, impressed by the thoroughness and fairness of the system: every shred of evidence was brought out and examined. The defence was aggressive but polite: much was made of how long it would take for a dog to become so emaciated and attempts were made to cast an element of doubt, because there is no hard data on emaciation in dogs based on clear science. But the evidence was clear. The court imposed a considerable fine, in keeping with the financial situation of the defendant, which would take her two years to pay off and she was banned from keeping dogs for five years. She was lucky: similar cases have led to life bans.

We soon found a new home for Lottie with a family and she is now being looked after well for the first time in her young life. It amazes me how quickly some animals seem to forget their suffering when they receive the proper level of care. But ·perhaps it isn't surprising: it's relatively easy to meet the pets' needs for love, security, good food, home comforts and exercise. Can anyone truly say that they love animals and not provide their pet with these basic necessities? It always saddens me when it is revealed in court how an animal has lacked them and, worse still, how very little insight defendants show when they find themselves facing prosecution. They *think* they love animals and that if they say this to the court they will be found not guilty.

Even more unsuitable owners than Brandy's and Lottie's are those horrible people involved in dog-fighting. I have dealt with such people many times but none so nasty as Michael A., J. F. and Al E. From the first time I met them I knew they were involved in some kind of business: they shared a passion for large American pitbull terriers of uncertain temperament. Their own personalities were similar: they were arrogant, rude and sometimes abusive and threatening, especially to the nurses. Often they would turn up at the emergency service late at night with injured dogs which should have been seen days earlier. Al E. seemed to specialise in rearing pitbull puppies. Over a year I saw several of his young dogs, who were never older than six months.

After yet another complaint from the nurses about verbal abuse, I went through the files on the three men. Three adult dogs belonging to them had been involved in a suspiciously large number of unprovoked dog attacks in the local park and each had been stitched up several times. Also, the dogs owned by Al E. seemed to become the property of the other men as they got older. I suspected a dog-fighting ring – but how could I prove it?

A few days later the answer provided itself when we had a visit from Ian G., who had worked as an ambulance driver before my time as the director of the hospital. He had trained as an RSPCA inspector and for a year had been working for the undercover group monitoring dog-fighting, illegal transport of animals and any other criminal activity that relies on surveillance to collect evidence. His visit was social but I asked his advice about the three men and if they could be followed.

Next day Ian phoned me to say that he had details on J. F., who had long been suspected of dog-fighting but had so far avoided being caught at raids. The world of dog-fighting was notoriously difficult to infiltrate, he told me, and not without some danger. Probably the best strategy would be to put all three under surveillance for a while and hope that they put a foot sufficiently wrong for the RSPCA to enlist the help of the police. Often a raid on these people's homes provides enough evidence to link them with dog-fighting and charges might be brought. Ian explained that these individuals are often involved in other crimes, especially drug-related, and sometimes their activities were brought to a halt by lengthy prison sentences.

We agreed that I would report any suspicions to him and he would update me on any developments over the coming months. I had a feeling that things would start to happen quickly since all three men had seemed to think that they were invulnerable to investigation. They had no idea how persistent we would be or, for that matter, how patient. Al E. had made me determined to investigate his activities by boasting openly that the situation was out of police control and that anyone could keep these dogs for protection or for whatever purpose they liked. I hoped that his arrogance would lead to carelessness and his own downfall, which would implicate his partners.

Over the years I had seen several people I suspected of being involved in dog-fighting. They always used American pitbull terriers and put the dogs through arduous physical training – for example, making them hang from a tree branch by their teeth. Once these dogs bite they will not let go and the owners would delight in recording how long they could remain motionless with their teeth embedded in a branch. Some dogs were also trained to pull enormous weights behind them to build up great strength. No one ever explained to me why this was necessary. These people were always polite to staff and took immense pains not to draw attention to themselves. One whom I had seen in private practice was eventually caught red-handed at a fight – or 'match', as it is termed. He received a sentence of six months in prison and had to pay a large fine, with costs. Now that the special investigations people were involved I hoped it would only be a matter of time before the same thing happened to the three men I had been seeing.

A weekend later the chance we were waiting for

presented itself. Late on Sunday evening Michael A. turned up with a pitbull in an appalling mess. The dog had obviously been involved in a fight – and no ordinary fight at that. He had multiple bite wounds all over his body and, in spite of intensive treatment, he died two hours after admission. Michael's story was the usual one: the dog had been set upon in the park, this time by a Doberman. He was his usual arrogant self, and told the vet who had tried to save his dog that she was incompetent. I notified Ian G. the next day. He told me our three suspects had met up a few days earlier and another suspected dog-fighter had been seen at Michael A.'s house. Plans were afoot for a raid. My news brought these plans forward, since Ian G. felt he might find further evidence of the most recent fight. The local police were now involved and a warrant was arranged to search the premises. The raid would take place on the following Wednesday morning after a dawn briefing. My role was to be at the hospital from 7.30 a.m. to await the arrival of any seized dogs. A police inspector, three RSPCA inspectors and half a dozen police offers were at the early-morning briefing. Reinforcements were to be called in the event of violence – which was a distinct possibility, given the record of the suspects.

At 6.51 a.m., Michael A. was woken and arrested on suspicion of contravening the Protection of Animals Act 1911. His mother was abusive although apparently Michael remained cocky and insolent, and refused to co-operate. Meanwhile the inspectors had to deal with the dogs. They found two pitbull terriers. One was a bitch in good condition, but the other, a male, had recent bite wounds. Both were put in the back of the RSPCA van. Meanwhile J. F. turned up. He had been alerted to the raid by phone and immediately launched into a diatribe against the police. He was told several times to be quiet and was arrested eventually for breach of the peace. Both men were taken to the police station for questioning.

Meanwhile, back at the hospital, I was examining the dogs. The bitch had been used for breeding – she had large pendulous teats. The male dog had bite wounds around the head and ears. None were serious but they were infected and painful to touch. Also, he had recently lost an upper canine tooth, which could only have happened from extreme trauma. Unless a veterinary surgeon could be found who had treated it – which was unlikely – I was confident that we had enough evidence already to secure a cruelty conviction, based on failure to provide the dog with treatment following injury.

At the police station both men had acquired solicitors and were being interviewed. Incriminating evidence had been found at the house: books on dog-fights and training methods for American pitbull terriers, photos of dog-fights and undeveloped film. A diary contained names and addresses, and huge studded collars, harnesses and a first-aid kit that included antibiotics. More sinister was the discovery of live bullets, although there was no gun.

After J. F.'s arrest a warrant had been issued to search his house and when police arrived they found another American pitbull bitch and nine puppies. The bitch was in very poor condition, covered in sores, and the pups weren't much better. They were seized and brought back to the hospital for further investigation. I found demodex mites on them, showing that the dog and her puppies had demodectic mange, and subsequent investigations proved that they had received no adequate treatment for more than three months. The dogs had been under the care of a friend of J. F., but he readily admitted who the true owner was. He was clearly terrified that the police would tell his friend that he had given them information. Evidently, like Michael A., J. F. had a reputation for violence.

I was pleased at the latest developments, and doubly so when one of the nurses recognised the bitch. When we went through our records, we discovered that she hadn't been seen for four months, which tied in nicely with the clinical findings. A day later Al E. was raided, but word had got to him and there were no dogs at his premises. Documentation showed that J. F.'s puppies had been destined for this address but there was no incriminating material that might lead to charges being laid. But there was no doubt that Al had had a fright. He couldn't do enough to distance himself from his erstwhile partners.

However, it was another year before the case came to court. Michael A. and J. F. were cautioned and charged with offences under the 1911 Act, then allowed bail. Neither attended the first hearing and warrants were issued for their arrest. In due course, J. F. was located and appeared for his trial. He claimed legal aid and was at first represented by a solicitor but, after heated discussions with her, he sacked her and elected to represent himself. He cross-examined every witness including me. His main defence seemed to be that the dogs were in good condition, had been well fed and had at some time received veterinary treatment. The photos and my evidence proved otherwise, though, to the satisfaction of the magistrates, and he was fined £500 with £1000 costs, and banned from keeping dogs for ten years. I thought he had got off lightly and evidently he did too, from the smile on his face. I had the impression that £1500 would not be difficult for him to find, given the likely nature of his business.

Meanwhile Michael A. had jumped bail and was believed to be in Cyprus, where he had right of abode. Inspector Ian G. had contacts who informed him that Michael was attempting to join the Cypriot Army. Some telephone calls to the Cypriot consul soon put paid to that, but we had to wait until he returned to the UK before he could be called to account for his activities. A network of informers was eager and waiting to 'grass' on him, if and when he made an appearance. Almost six months to the day later he was seen at one of his old haunts. Within twenty-four hours he was picked up at another dawn raid and placed in custody.

Like his friend he decided to defend himself and cross-examined me as to the physical condition of the dog that had been fighting. His appearance was chilling – he looked rather like a 1930s gangster. He had no insight into animal suffering and thought that the dogs enjoyed a good fight. The basis of his defence was that the dog was in good physical condition – he ignored the injuries. I had to say that the dog was physically fit and he tried then to persuade the magistrates that because it was well fed there could have been no cruelty. When the six months' prison sentence and life-time ban on keeping dogs was handed out he showed no remorse and threw contemptuous, angry looks at me.

With the removal of these three undesirable characters, the hospital seemed quieter and the number of pitbull terriers we saw plummeted. I hasten to add that not all of the pitbulls we see are owned by unsuitable people: many are well loved and docile but they should all be kept under close control and never allowed to get into a scrap since the other dog always comes off second best.

I never saw either Michael A. or J. F. after their court appearances, but about six months later J. F. was stabbed to death in a fight over drug deals. I had not known that apparently he always carried a knife tucked into his trousers. I finally understood why everyone who knew him was so wary of him. A few months later Michael A. was caught red-handed by the police in an armed robbery. Now we knew the significance of the live bullets that had been found in the RSPCA raid. For this he was sentenced to nine years in prison.

It isn't always deliberate cruelty to an animal that lands someone in court. Sometimes a moment's thoughtlessness is enough. Susie, a ten-year-old poodle, was the pride and joy of her owner, who took her little dog with her to work every day. Emma had had Susie since she was a teenager taking her A levels and since she had left university and got a job, the two had been inseparable.

One Sunday afternoon Emma had travelled up from south London to visit a college friend, who had asthma. Before she went into her friend's house, she took Susie for a walk round the park, then left her in the car. It was a hot, sultry afternoon but the sun wasn't out and she had left the car in a shady spot with the windows slightly open. She was going to stay only a short time, and had thought there would be no problem. But Emma and her friend had lots to talk about and an hour and a half flew by before Emma thought of Susie and went down to the car to check.

She could see something was wrong as soon as she got into the street. A small crowd had gathered round her car and two police cars had pulled alongside. With a terrible feeling of blind panic she rushed to the car. A policeman had already broken into it and Susie was in one of the police cars, which shot off as Emma arrived. Another policeman asked, 'Is this your car, madam?' Emma could only nod through the tears. 'The dog is on its way to the RSPCA, and an inspector will want to interview you.' The sun had come up and the shade in which Emma had parked her car was gone. The temperature inside it must have been in the nineties. Every year, despite publicity campaigns, people make the sometimes fatal mistake of leaving an animal in a car.

The first I knew of any of this was when the police car roared up. The police often bring animals to us: it is a part of their work that the public rarely see or find out about. The sight of a police car arriving in the car park usually signals an emergency and the staff went straight out to it.

Susie was in a bad way, collapsed and panting furiously. In spite of this her tongue was blue. I took her temperature and within seconds it was near the top of the scale – more than 106°F. Heat stroke. We see far too many of these cases, but at least that means we know exactly what to do. Susie's head was put under a cold tap while I inserted an airway into her windpipe and started her on pure oxygen. Then she had injections of respiratory and heart stimulants, steroids to reduce any swelling of the brain tissue and sedatives to dilate the blood vessels. I worked on her for an hour but had difficulty in getting her temperature down quickly so I immersed her briefly in ice-cold water. After that we monitored Susie's temperature until it was down to 103°. Her colour didn't improve much and she was only just conscious so I set up a drip to protect the blood circulation and try to ward off shock.

By now two hours had passed and I began to fear the worst: there was a distinct possibility of permanant brain damage because Susie's temperature was still so high. Emma told me, between sobs, that Susie was under treatment for a heart murmur, which caused a cough. I had listened to her heart but it was racing so fast that I couldn't detect a murmur – which is a sign of leaky heart valves.

There was little else we could do but wait and hope. Emma stayed in the hospital while we continued to battle for the life of her dog. At about nine in the evening Susie turned the corner: she was sleeping peacefully and, most importantly, her breathing was much easier. Her colour had returned to a healthy pink and her temperature was normal. She would survive. The next day she was fit to go home, seemingly none the worse for her ordeal. Emma was tearful with relief but was lucky that, in view of the mitigating circumstances, she only received a verbal caution.

It may seem from what you have read so far that dogs are the animals most commonly treated cruelly, but many cases are taken each year to court by the RSPCA involving other species, from horses and farm animals to cats and birds – in fact, any creature that can be kept by humans. Yet it is only a small minority who face prosecution, and real deliberate cruelty is rare. I am quite sure that without the RSPCA as a watchdog the level would be much higher. Equally, compared with many other countries, Britain has much to be proud of as far as general care of animals is concerned. Education is the key to achieving the fundamental aim of the RSPCA, which is the prevention of cruelty to animals.

Never a week goes by without several animals turning up at the hospital in urgent need of a loving owner. It's one of the hardest aspects of working at the Harmsworth and you have to learn quickly that you can't take them all home or even find them a home with someone else as the numbers are so great. I am sure that if I had unlimited money or a very large house – I haven't! – I would end up with an enormous array of rescue animals. But however sensible we try to be, there's always one special case which gets through the barriers we put up. Mine was Barney.

Few dogs could have had a worse start in life than

Barney. He had been let loose on the streets of south London to fend for himself and had not been very good at it. The inevitable road accident had occurred. The night he was run over I was on duty in a private practice in south London. We had received a call from the police saying that they had picked up an injured puppy from the gutter and they volunteered to bring him in. Shortly afterwards one of the largest policemen I have ever seen arrived, holding a little puppy in the palm of his hand. In spite of having a severely broken leg the puppy was wagging his tail. He was one of those dogs – Dalmatians are a good example – that grin when they are pleased to see someone and Barney was grinning hard at me. If anything, he looked like a German shepherd cross. I never did figure out exactly what he was crossed with – perhaps a beagle, because I found out later that one of his specialities was to wander off in a distracted way sniffing everything, and if you looked at his body and ignored his head he looked like a beagle. Even experienced breeders, and I asked plenty over the years, weren't quite sure what he was. But whatever his breed the treatment seemed simple enough: get him over the shock of the accident and then ship him off to the RSPCA to see what they could do for him. The next day an inspector called into the practice and took him to the hospital in Putney. I didn't rate his prospects highly as it can be difficult to find good homes for healthy pups, let alone those with broken legs. But puppies are good at selling themselves and Barney excelled at that. In spite of everything, he adored people and his eyes shone with devotion. And, of course, there was that grin.

A few days later I heard more of Barney. Apparently his charm had endeared him to everyone in the Putney hospital. The night after his operation to fix the broken leg he had slept in the ambulance drivers' quarters and never went back into a cage. He stayed with the drivers for a few days, successive shifts caring for him. But he couldn't stay with them for ever and was sent to the Battersea Dogs' Home in case his original owners were looking for him – unlikely – but otherwise to find him a new home.

It was at Battersea that our paths crossed again. Part of my job in private practice consisted of checking all the animals in the dogs' home two or three times a week and one afternoon I walked in to find a nurse watching a little pup who I recognised straight away as Barney. He was sitting on the floor trying to scratch his ear with his bad leg. All the time he was gazing up at the nurse and wagging his tail. As I walked in she said, 'Isn't this the dog that was treated at your practice?'

'What are his chances?' I asked. The nurse looked at me, it was obvious what she was thinking.

For some time I had been considering getting a dog and I wanted a rescue dog, but an adult not a puppy and certainly not one with a broken leg. I thought for a moment, then said that I wanted an adult dog.

But Barney was still on my mind and that evening I discussed him with my wife. Taking him on would mean a lot of hard work with no guaranteed success, especially as he was a puppy and needed a phenomenal amount of care and training. Even so adult dogs are much harder to rehome than puppies, which is why I had been thinking on those lines. My wife said that she would like to meet Barney and we agreed that she would accompany me on my next visit to Battersea at the end of the week.

That Friday afternoon we arrived at the dogs' home a little early. When we went into the clinic we found Barney on the table, looking sick and dejected. He had developed a severe form of kennel cough, his leg wasn't improving and he was about to be put to sleep. It was felt that his chances of being rehomed were minimal, which was why the difficult decision had been taken. I looked at my wife and that was it. I picked him up and said, 'After all he's been through we can't have this. Let's get him home.' And that was that.

He sat on my wife's lap coughing all the way home and there followed several anxious weeks. He needed intensive nursing, and just as he started to get over the cough he developed the potentially fatal parvo-virus infection. It took five days of day-and-night nursing, fluids and antibiotics before he turned the corner and started to eat. Even then he wasn't out of the woods. Further operations were necessary on his leg and it was three months before I could say that at last he was cured, on the day we removed his stitches from the latest operation.

For his first real outing we took him to Eastbourne on a nice sunny day. He was still limping and I was scolded by an irate lady, who told me to take him to a vet or she would report me to the RSPCA! I didn't tell her that he had already had the best possible treatment.

Barney was a real survivor, and within weeks he was playing in the park with the other dogs, running, twisting and turning like a rugby three-quarter. This became one of his specialities: he could make a chasing dog run the wrong way, which was very funny to watch. What a transformation. It took two years of patient training to turn him into the wonderful dog he became. First he went through a chewing phase whenever he was left alone. Then he liked to tip over the rubbish bin and investigate the contents. And there was the fun and games in the park: his favourite trick was to clear off with the other dogs and not come back until the whistling got to a frantic pitch. Then he would pause, look, and clearly decide whether to come back at that point, or – more usually – to carry on playing. I realised quickly that it was pointless to get annoyed and shout at him: he was having fun and wouldn't understand why he was being told off. One way to get his instant attention was with food which, next to racing around in the park, was his greatest joy and we taught him to come back to us by rewarding him with his favourite dog biscuits. Eventually he became a faithful companion, who went everywhere with me and gave unconditional love to everyone he met.

If you plan to have a pet, do think seriously about rehoming one rather than buying one from a pet shop, or a breeder. The rewards of giving a happy home to a stray or an animal that has had a bad start in life are potentially so great. Barney became a real member of our family and taking him home all those years ago was one of the best things I have ever done.

CHAPTER FOUR

Surgery

Most days, except on Wednesdays when I see skin cases, I get involved with surgery, which takes place in the preparation room – called the prep room or just PR – and the two operating theatres. The prep room is really the engine room of the hospital and is always frantically busy with minor procedures like dentals, stitch-ups and blood sampling. Anaesthetics are given here before an animal goes into theatre, and it is where the innumerable accidents and emergencies are assessed and receive their preliminary treatment. When new vets join the hospital I always start them in the prep room for the first week to accustom them to the pace at which we have to work but also to learn hospital procedures and get to know everyone – we all pop in to there at some point every day. Andrea, our newest vet from New Zealand, said at the end of her first day, 'This place is like *ER*!

It's a fact that you never know what's going to come through the door next. At busy times three vets and three nurses will be here or in one of the theatres, and also a nurse team, consisting of a fully qualified nurse plus a trainee performing minor procedures ranging from blood taking to changing plaster-of-paris supports. It's an exciting place to be but stressful, and we try to ensure that everyone gets a mid-morning break for coffee of at least twenty minutes and an hour for lunch before the hectic afternoon.

The operating theatres are often a haven of peace and quiet, where you can get on with an operation, usually without too much interruption. Even so, important phone calls always seem to come in for me once I have scrubbed up but I have resisted getting a phone with a loudspeaker as this would mean no peace at all! The theatres are spacious enough to make you feel at ease, with air conditioning in the summer.

Keeping the surgery list manageable can be difficult. Typically we'll do up to ten major operations in a day, with sometimes another thirty minor ones mainly performed in the prep room. Also, we will need to X-ray four or five other animals, which is almost always done under general anaesthetic as the animal must be perfectly still on the X-ray plate. The person taking the

X-ray stands behind a lead screen to push the button and a red light on the door outside warns everyone not to come in while this is going on.

The final part of prep-room work is the clinical examination of all the animals not dealt with on the ward round because their condition is complicated and needs detailed assessment. Small wonder that when we are in this area of the hospital the time flies past. You can be continually on the go from eight thirty in the morning until five thirty in the afternoon but a day here can seem like half an hour, particularly when RTAs – road traffic accidents – are piling through the door.

We have to be wary about filming in the prep room because so much work is done here that we can get disastrously behind if there is disruption. When we first began filming vets became desperate to get on with their work as they waited for a final take. BBC producers are perfectionists and when they have only a few cameras to work with they like to film as many takes as they can of each sequence, perhaps as many as half a dozen. This makes for a high standard of programme but we discovered that it was essential for us to negotiate times of filming: I found it easiest for the BBC researchers to agree filming times with the theatre supervisor, and from that we learned that putting the supervisor in charge of operation admissions went a long way to improving list numbers. When we all booked in for ourselves, we sometimes became far too busy and had to cancel operations. We still have to resort to that, if a vet goes off sick, but owners are normally understanding.

The most common emergencies to pass through the prep room result from road accidents, and cats are particularly prone to being hurt this way. It is one of the disadvantages of keeping a cat in London but even in remote country areas, wherever there is traffic in fact, cats are run over. The majority are less than a year old and every year we see hundreds with all manner of injuries. Broken bones and smashed pelvises are the most common and all vets in city practice soon become experienced in traumatology. But nothing prepares you for a serious accident involving your own cat.

Before my wife and I moved house we rejected several possibilities on the grounds that Penny, our cat, would be unlikely to survive long anywhere near a main road. We were pleased when we found a suitable house with a nice garden in a crescent with little through traffic. For the first couple of years it was perfect, and Penny settled in well. She had had a rough start in life, having been abandoned in a poor part of London in a built-up area. Out of curiosity my wife and I visited the road where she had been found: it was busy with no greenery and a bit depressing. As I watched the cars speeding along I knew why Penny had always been terrified of traffic, and why it had taken her a couple of years to gain confidence when she came to live with us.

When I became director of the Harmsworth, we lived for the first seven years in south London. We had a small, reasonably secluded garden, and Penny didn't stray far. Later we moved to north London, which made life much easier. Travelling across London in rush-hour traffic every day is no fun. For the first year everything was perfect. We had a bigger house and Penny seemed even happier than she had been before. Cats, as any owner will tell you, appreciate home comforts and the bigger the garden the more there is to explore. Our new garden was three times the size of the old one and Penny loved it. Therein lay the seeds of her downfall. By nature cats are curious and as Penny's confidence grew so her boundaries extended. Several times on the way to work I spotted her a couple of hundred yards away from home and near a cut-through favoured by speeding cars. Short of keeping her in, there was not much I could do but hope that as she was now six years old she might have enough sense to keep out of trouble. However, she was constantly challenging the cat next door, called – aptly – Rocky. When it came to fighting Rocky was in a different league so Penny usually lost out. We never saw much in the way of injury because Penny tended to run when things got too hot.

The day of her accident my wife found Penny crawling painfully up the garden, her face a mass of blood. Her right eye had come out of its socket and her jaw seemed to be broken. She restrained her in a basket and phoned the hospital. I had been about to come home when I got the news and immediately a couple of nurses went on standby for emergency surgery. I headed off home to find Penny in a very sorry state. I injected her with some painkiller and set off with her straight back to the hospital. The nurses had a drip set up almost as I walked through the door and we prepared the theatre for a lengthy operation.

It wasn't until I got Penny under an anaesthetic that

the true extent of her injuries became evident. She had lost her right eye and the remnants would have to be removed. Her jaw was broken badly in two places and had been pushed back a couple of inches, dislocating it. But the worst injury of all was to her nose, which had become separated from the hard palate. She was an appalling mess. I started by dealing with the eye – a relatively simple job. Then I repaired her jaw with strong nylon sutures and, with a struggle, replaced it back in the proper joints. Finally I stitched her nose back into place. The whole operation took two hours and at the end of it I was exhausted. Throughout it I had been so wrapped up in working out how best to sort out the injuries that I had no time to reflect that I was operating on my wife's cat whom she had rescued and to whom she was devoted. I could not bring myself to talk about it afterwards, but the whole operation was filmed.

Initially I found it daunting to be filmed during surgery. If an operation was particularly interesting at least three cameras would be in the theatre. Two would be set up and I, or whichever vet was operating, would spend some time advising the director where the animal would be lying before giving the anaesthetic so that the cameras could be positioned correctly. A third camera would be stationed on the operating lamp for a bird's eye view. With producers, cameras, lighting and sound people around it didn't pay to look up during the operation, but I soon found that all those people didn't hinder me – in fact their presence tended to increase my concentration and again, just as with the consultations, a sufficient number of cameras meant that I rarely had to repeat procedures – which is what most people find so irritating with film crews.

When I was working on Penny, though, the operation was filmed on one hand-held camera. The cameraman, Barry, is a superb technician and I was simply not aware of him. When the film was reviewed, it was clear that he had achieved what was normally only possible with all three cameras. And I admired his physical strength – those cameras are heavy!

The last thing I had to do for Penny before taking her to the ward was to insert a naso-gastric tube, through which she would have to be fed for the next week or so, and give her another shot of powerful painkiller for when she came round. I left her in the hands of the nurses, who checked her through the night and gave her another injection in the early hours, then I went home and straight to bed.

Penny is not the easiest cat to nurse. Apart from her poor beginnings, she is also a tortoiseshell – they're lovely cats but can be a little temperamental. For the first two days it was touch and go, and then on the third day she began to improve. Meanwhile a couple of the nurses had got round her and she was letting them do the tube feeding without kicking up too much fuss. Also she was having to cope with twice daily injections of strong antibiotics and painkillers, and this went on for some weeks. It was a hard battle, and I felt for her, but there was nothing to be done except persevere and wait for the healing process to take its course.

After two weeks I came in to see written on her card 'Penny is eating on her own!' Trudy, one of the nurses to whom Penny had taken a liking, had tempted her to feed without the tube. When this happens, progress is usually rapid and I took out the tube and removed the collar that prevented her from interfering with it. These collars are essential but cats hate them and the simple act of removing them leads to a visible lightening of mood and it wasn't long before I was able to take Penny home. For the first month she refused to leave the house and was as timid as she had been when she was first rescued. Also, she remained on continuous antibiotics because the turbinate bones – tiny honeycomb-like bones in the nose – had become infected due to the accident and contamination. Gradually her confidence came back and she started to go out more or less as she had before. Strangely, though, since the accident she and Rocky seemed to have called a truce. I suspect that Penny's notorious stubbornness had weakened and she had finally accepted Rocky as the dominant cat.

Although outdoor cats are always in danger of road accidents, when I saw Penny climbing our pear tree or sleeping upside down at its foot I knew she was in cat heaven and that is was worth the risk of letting her out. And an indoor cat is never entirely safe. Every summer we see an average of six cats a week which have fallen from great heights. Amazingly, many survive.

The injuries are similar. In most cases, if the unfortunate cat lands forefeet first, both front legs may be broken and almost invariably the jaw. If the jaw is broken, the inside of the mouth, particularly the hard palate is split. These cats need intensive treatment. First the broken legs have to be fixed, usually with plates and screws, then the palate is sutured and a naso-gastric tube inserted as feeding is too painful. This simple technique has revolutionised our care of these cases, but even so a hospital stay of two weeks or more is normal. We reckon that if the cats arrive alive at the hospital we can save the majority. Those that land back feet first are slightly better off, although they usually break both shin bones, which have to be pinned. This may sound terrible but cats with fractures often do well and are walking within a few weeks after a stay of perhaps a week. The sad thing is that these accidents are easily preventable: all you need to do is rig up some netting across open windows in tower blocks when the weather is warm. I wanted to try to publicise the misery of cats who fall from high places to try to prevent similar accidents, and during the first series of *Animal Hospital*, I told the producers to expect large numbers of these cases if the weather turned hot. Within a few days we had eight and decided to feature the next one on the programme.

We didn't have to wait long. The same day, late in the afternoon, Candy was rushed in. She was only ten weeks old and had survived a multi-storey fall. She arrived in a pitiful state, in shock and pain. I checked her jaw, palate and front limbs. All intact. But when I examined her rear end I found both femurs broken. Poor little thing – no wonder she was in such pain. I immediately gave her a painkilling injection and the nurses set up a drip to counteract the shock. Next I took some X-rays to confirm what I already knew, but also to assess the extent of the damage. Both femurs had nasty breaks near the knee joint and there was a lot of displacement – the broken bone ends were far apart

– which meant that we would have to operate sooner rather than later. Jeremy was on duty and he operated throughout the evening.

Meanwhile Candy's plight had been shown on live television and the phones erupted with people wanting to know the outcome, which was far from certain as Jeremy set about repairing her injuries. The operation took several hours, with constant filming, and was eventually completed at about 10.30 p.m. Four metal pins had been inserted in Candy's legs and, heavily sedated and full of painkiller, she was handed over to the nurses who would take care of her through the night. The resilience of animals, particularly the young, never ceases to amaze me: the next day on my ward rounds Candy was purring and wanting food.

Ten million people witnessed our fight to save Candy and it certainly concentrated the minds of those who had indoor cats. Over the next three months we had only two or three more cases of high-rise syndrome – as the Americans call it. I reckon we prevented at least eighty cats in the London area from suffering a similar fate and goodness knows how many in the country as a whole. But the next summer we saw an increasing number of cases: the public's memory is short. One injured cat had been in the flat only two hours after arriving from the pet shop. This is part of our job, a never-ending journey of education, but the power of television to do good is awe-inspiring. We need these programmes all year round.

I find it intriguing that it is mostly cats that fall out of high-rise buildings but road accidents aren't exclusive to them. One Sunday morning, a Mr

Papadopoulos appeared with his dog, Rebel, a beautiful, and enormous, German shepherd. The dog had been hit by a car and both he and his owner were very shocked – as was the driver. Rebel was in great pain and was put straight on a drip and given painkillers to stabilise him before I assessed the extent of the damage. We gave Mr Papadopoulos a cup of tea to calm him and got to work on his dog.

The accident was typical of many. Although he was normally good in traffic, Rebel had seen a cat on the other side of the road and couldn't resist the chase. Unfortunately for him, although it was a quiet Sunday morning the only car that happened to be on the road at that moment hit him. It had been travelling at some speed so we could expect fractures, and as Rebel had been hit in the rear I would need to concentrate on his hind legs.

I found that the dog's left hind leg was injured and the pain he showed when I touched his hip indicated exactly where the problem lay. I had a feeling that, as far as the dog was concerned, this would be a straightforward case. I suspected a dislocated hip and when Rebel had come out of shock I gave him an anaesthetic so that we could take some X-rays. Sure enough, as soon as the plates were developed I saw the dislocated hip. If this injury is caught early, replacing the hip is usually easy.

The next thing to do was to transfer the dog on to an anaesthetic machine. He needed to be deeply unconscious for me to be able to slip the hip back into place easily because it is only in this state that the muscles relax. As Rebel was such a large dog I would need all my strength for the manoeuvre. I started to manipulate the joint around six hours after the accident. After I had pulled, pushed and rotated it for a while there was a sudden, huge *clunk* as it went back into position. I still love that sound, even after many years of hearing it: it tells me that, in all probability, the dog will make a complete recovery without needing surgery – and complicated surgery at that. And, of course, the pain will have been virtually abolished. When Rebel came round, about three-quarters of an hour later, he was visited by his tearful owner: a wag of the tail was all the proof he needed that his dog was on the mend.

The next day, an enormous box of chocolates was delivered to the nurses, and the day after that Rebel was fit to leave. In any case he had signalled his desire to go home several hours earlier with a theatrical howl. Normally I like to keep dislocated-hip cases in for three or four days but after Mr Papadopoulos had assured me that Rebel would get plenty of rest we let him go. There were more tears on their reunion, and I was pleased to see that Rebel now had a nice new lead. He wouldn't have another accident like that.

A final check a week later showed continued good progress in Rebel and we signed him off.

Although a lot of the injuries we see are common, something unusual or interesting is always round the corner. Blue was a Russian Blue cat, aged just over a year and I was in the prep room away from the hurly-burly of the clinic and my office with its mountain of paperwork and incessant phone calls. I couldn't decide what operation to do out of the many seemingly routine options on the list so I asked the nurse to pick one. With an eye to the approaching coffee break, she suggested we stitch up Blue – a fifteen minute job in all probability.

While I was preparing the anaesthetic I cast an eye over Blue's clinic record and saw that she had been admitted last night with a large wound on her back. A dressing had been put in but the stitch-up was postponed until the morning as she had not long eaten and it would be risky to place her under anaesthetic. It struck me suddenly that this was the third time Blue had needed a stitch-up in her short life. She certainly seemed accident prone.

A few minutes later, when the cat was sleeping quietly, Sue, the nurse, took off the dressing. Immediately the wound split and doubled in size. So much for fifteen minutes – we now had a major job on our hands. I began the laborious task of putting in the thirty or so stitches that would be needed. 'I'll show you something when we've finished this,' I said to Sue, and also asked for my camera to be brought down from my office.

I was pretty sure that Blue was suffering from a rare skin disease that had been present from birth and which makes the skin elasticity seventeen times weaker than it should be. The skin in these animals stretches to unbelievable lengths but also tears easily, leaving large, gaping wounds, which normally heal rapidly, though scars tend to develop. While I was explaining this to Sue I pointed out scars from previous wounds. I had only seen the condition once before in all my time as a vet and that had been in a dog.

Sue noticed that I was putting in large 'mattress' stitches. They aren't very elegant but they don't easily split or pull out – necessary considerations with such fragile skin. I took a skin sample and put it in formalin so that it could be processed in a lab and examined by a histopathologist, who would hopefully confirm my diagnosis. 'Now watch this,' I said to Sue, and gently pulled on the skin of the cat's cheeks. It stretched right out, looking quite bizarre. I had photos taken of this and also showing how the skin on the animal's back could be lifted up way beyond the norm. The disease, I told Sue, was called Ehlers Danlos syndrome. I just hoped that the photos would come out so that I could add them to my collection of skin conditions, which I have been making for fifteen years. Now I have almost every condition on file.

Blue made an uneventful recovery and was soon on her way home. I made an appointment to see the owners in ten days: by then the stitches would be ready to come out and the results of the biopsy should be to hand. Ehlers Danlos syndrome is a disorder of the collagen bundles in the dermis, the part of the skin which nourishes and supports it as a whole, and this can normally be seen in stained sections. Ten days later the diagnosis was confirmed and I was talking to the owners while I gently removed the stitches.

First I told them the good news, that this condition is not fatal, then came the bad part, which was that Blue would be much better off permanently indoors to minimise the possibility of tearing her skin while climbing trees or getting into scraps with other cats. If something happened in the home it would be immediately apparent and could be dealt with. Even so, it was likely that further wounds would occur and would need prompt stitch-ups. Fortunately the wounds don't seem to be painful and bleed very little. Some owners give up after the third or fourth episode and, on grounds of cost, have their cat put to sleep. I was sure that Blue's owners would not fall into this category: they were already discussing how to make their home safer. They were a retired couple and they commented on how it took them back to when they had young children and had to think of all the possible dangers lurking in the house.

Blue was fortunate to have good owners and it was a year before his next accident occurred when a grandson, a toddler, grabbed her clumsily while everybody's back was turned, on Christmas Day of all days! By chance I was on duty and, dissatisfied with my original photos of Blue's skin, took some more, to the amusement of the nurses who felt that at Christmas I should give it a rest. We sent Blue home for the rest of Christmas but told her owners to keep her in temporary isolation until the family had gone home. We haven't seen her since but I received a Christmas card the following year to say all was well.

Although conditions like Ehlers Danlos syndrome are interesting, they are rare. Cancer, on the other hand, is very common and its treatment is now an important part of every vet's life. It can occur in any part of the body but in cats and dogs it is particularly common in the skin and I have made a study of skin tumours. A week never goes by when I don't operate to remove a skin tumour, mostly in dogs, in which the incidence of skin tumours is three to four times that of cats. I usually take photos of the tumour and send the tissue for confirmation of the diagnosis, then take pictures of the tissue under the microscope.

One Monday morning I arrived to find three possible cancer cases that needed surgery and as everyone else was on holiday I was the only vet in theatre. After ward rounds I settled down to a morning of oncology, as the study of cancerous growths is known. The first patient was Chalky, a seventeen-year-old white cat with a cancerous ear tip. This would almost certainly be a squamous cell carcinoma, a malignant tumour, which fortunately spreads only after a very long time so rarely causes death. I find it satisfying to operate on these as there is such a good prospect of cure. This type of tumour is undoubtedly on the increase and is the second most common cancer that I find in cats. I well remember more than twenty-five years ago when I first saw a case: finding it hard to believe that the disease could exist in England. It has always been known that this cancer is caused by sunlight and England then was never associated with much of that! Perhaps it occurs now because the ozone layer is thinner. My first case was in a twenty-year-old cat, whose age was then a rarity, but is now not uncommon. This tumour always affects white-haired skin which doesn't have the protecting pigment melanin.

Chalky had an angry-looking bleeding ulcer on the end of one of his ears, which on closer inspection, I could see appeared to have been eaten away. It was causing him some discomfort and he was constantly scratching at it. I had discussed the operation with his owner, Jane, a music student at one of the London colleges. Chalky had grown up with her and she didn't want him to spend his remaining days separated from her. At seventeen there was no knowing how many were left to him. When she heard the dreaded word cancer Jane felt that putting him to sleep might be the best answer. Should he be put through the operation? How long might he survive if he was? These were the very reasonable questions she asked me.

A careful clinical examination revealed Chalky to be robustly healthy apart from his ear. I thought the outlook for a cure was good but although there would be a slightly increased anaesthetic risk due to his age and I couldn't say how long he would live afterwards. The actual operation would be simple and Jane could expect the wound to heal within ten days. She agreed to the surgery, which we scheduled for the following Monday. I caught a glimpse of her leaving the hospital, after Chalky had been admitted. She was crying and obviously fearing the worst, so I decided to make the operation the first of the day.

After a bit of a fight, we had Chalky under the anaesthetic. As cats get older they may become cantankerous and nowhere is this better demonstrated than when you try to give them an anaesthetic. The gentle purring creature of the consulting room becomes, without his owner, a snarling beast all teeth and claws. In spite of a tranquillising injection, Chalky got me within seconds, first with his claws and then with one of his few remaining teeth. I rolled him up in a large towel and managed to get an injection into his vein, his protests ringing in my ears. Then all that I had to do was remove the tumour with sharp scissors and carefully stitch skin to skin over the cartilage of the ear. It took less than twenty minutes. I left a note for the nurses that once he had come round he was to have a collar on his head so that he couldn't scratch out the sutures. The removed tissue was sent off for confirmation of diagnosis at the laboratory. Finally I gave him a painkilling injection, whose effects would last for the next twenty-four hours, and an antibiotic. Quite a good start to the morning, and we had time for another operation before coffee.

This was to be Sofia, a large German shepherd dog who had reached fourteen without a day's illness and then had suddenly slowed down. She had also developed an obvious swelling in her tummy. The family had thought it was due to old age and had not come to the hospital until Sofia had started refusing to go for walks. When I examined the dog, I found a large hard mass in the abdomen, which was confirmed on X-ray. In this breed the most likely diagnosis was cancer of the spleen and we arranged to do an exploratory operation. I had already instituted a full series of blood tests and an X-ray of Sofia's chest, which showed no abnormalities and it didn't seem that the tumour had spread. The tests were important: the operation would be a big one and I needed to be sure that it was likely to prolong Sofia's life.

I began the operation and five minutes later the spleen was in full view. It was at least three times its normal size. I eased it out, then looked at the liver, an obvious site for early spread. Nothing was visible, which was a good sign – at least in the short term. Ahead of me now lay the laborious task of locating all the blood vessels supplying such a large organ and tying them off so that I could remove it. An hour later we were finished and Sofia was doing remarkably well – she regained consciousness just as I put in the last stitch. I decided to keep her in hospital for a day or so, watching for any sign of bleeding, then send her home. Her owners had already been on the phone twice during the day and I knew she would get VIP nursing at home.

I sent off a piece of the spleen for examination, thinking that it would probably turn out to be a cancer called haemangiosarcoma. I had to know for sure, though, as it would tell us the long-term risk of spread. Unfortunately these tumours have a habit of spreading to the lungs and causing death some months later, even if at the time of operation there was no sign of spread on the X-ray. We would have to wait and see.

Now to the final operation of the morning. I swapped nurses to allow for coffee breaks and decided to work on myself since I had a meeting in the afternoon and would not be in the hospital. In any case, I thought, the operation was going to be quite quick. Jazz was a retired racing greyhound now getting on for nine years old. Over a period of about six months she had developed a tremendous swelling in her abdomen, rather like Sofia's. But Jazz's owners had waited too long before bringing her in: by the time I came to look at her she was in poor condition. Although she weighed 75 pounds, she was quite thin and having trouble breathing. The huge lump in her tummy seemed to occupy the whole space. Again the dilemma: should I put her to sleep? Was there any point in trying to remove the growth, whatever it was? Would she survive? And if so, for how long? Were these owners sufficiently motivated? I had my doubts, at least initially, because they'd left the tumour untreated. But in the end I could see that they cared very much for their dog. I thought that in all probability the operation would merely establish the inoperable nature of a large cancer. However, within ten minutes I realised that this was going to be anything but quick. As I opened the abdomen it became apparent that I was dealing with a cancer of the womb. I found the ovaries, which were normal – a good sign as cancers of the ovaries are frequently very malignant and nothing can be done. Cancers of the womb are rare but sometimes quite benign, which means that they don't spread and kill and can be cured if the womb is removed, which became the object of the exercise over the next hour and a half. The main problem was the sheer size of it. I had to make a cut from the dog's breastbone to the end of her abdomen. Even then it was a struggle to lift out the mass and I had to bring in a nurse to help. She scrubbed up and held the womb while I tied off all the blood vessels and lifted it out. Later we weighed it: 25 pounds, the heaviest I have come across. This meant that Jazz now weighed only 50 pounds, and was some 15 pounds underweight.

Stitching up was a long, laborious process. First innumerable stitches in the muscle layers, then forty or so in the skin. I checked out her colour at the end, which was surprisingly good – greyhounds are very tough. Finally, as in the other two operations of the morning, I sent off material to check on the type of tumour.

A week later I had the results and probable outcome in all three cases. Chalky's cancer was confirmed as a squamous cell carcinoma with an excellent outlook. Jazz had been suffering from a benign tumour of the womb and should therefore be considered cured. However, Sofia's tumour was confirmed as a haemangiosarcoma, and the outlook for her was guarded. Nevertheless she went on to reach her fifteenth birthday before developing heart failure and passing away peacefully, and quite suddenly, one night. When I think back on that morning I can still feel the satisfaction of having cured animals whose owners were in despair, but cancer in animals, as well as in humans, does not necessarily bring with it a death sentence.

The other satisfaction in surgery comes from performing either very complex operations successfully or relatively straightforward ones where you know the outcome is likely to be a full recovery. One of my favourites is a cystotomy, which means opening the bladder. It was the first major operation I had to do when I first worked at the Harmsworth as a young, recently qualified vet.

Although I knew the theory well enough, I needed the support of my nurse, Mary, who must have seen literally hundreds of similar cases. She monitored the anaesthetic and kept an eye on me too, making encouraging noises and telling me that I was doing the operation just as well as my boss would have done it. This was a slight exaggeration, of course, as he had been qualified twenty-four years and could have done it in half the time, but I can still remember every detail of the case now and of the subsequent operation.

It was a mixed breed dog called Cassie, who was owned by Mr and Mrs Molloy, a retired couple. She was eight years old and for a couple of weeks had been having trouble urinating. On her walks she would go quite a few times but never pass much, then suddenly her owners saw her pass a little blood. I had been at the hospital only a few weeks, and I thought to start with that Cassie had cystitis, or inflammation of the bladder. I felt her tummy, but she tensed up and growled so I abandoned that part of the examination. Then I had a choice: I could either admit her for a full investigation or treat her with antibiotics and see if she responded. I elected to do the latter since we had a full list that afternoon. If she didn't respond to the treatment we could always do the investigation in a few days' time. It is a pragmatic approach that I still adopt today because it is impossible to do a complete investigation of every case at first examination. As a vet you wear two hats every day: the GP's, which involves sorting out cases and deciding whether they need to be in hospital, and the specialist's, which means diagnosing difficult cases and, if necessary, operating. It makes for great variety.

Often the clinical hunch is correct and the animal quickly gets better with drug treatment but in Cassie's case it wasn't. Four days later when her owners brought her back I was leafing through the operations book to see when I could fit her in for an X-ray and possible exploratory cystotomy. Although she seemed brighter, her owners said, she looked uncomfortable and was squatting interminably when out for a walk. They were due to go on holiday in three weeks' time and were worried that they would have to cancel as no one would be able to look after Cassie. They were planning to go to Ireland to visit Mr Molloy's father, who was to celebrate his ninety-second birthday. I admitted Cassie for investigation the next day.

Cassie was a gentle and loving dog who would let you do anything to her, except touch her sore tummy, without even a murmur so I laid her on her side and took an X-ray of her bladder as a starting point. As Mary developed the X-ray, I heard her shout, 'It's got stones!' and, sure enough, lying neatly in the centre of the bladder were three beauties. Large, smooth, round bladder stones.

'We can do this after lunch, if you like,' Mary said. 'You're in theatre, aren't you?' She knew I was as she was the theatre supervisor.

'Right,' was all I could think of saying, and I spent the lunch hour refreshing my mind as to the details of the operation.

I was perfectly capable of performing a cystotomy, I reminded myself. In the short time I had been at the Harmsworth I had already done several minor ops. And in any case two other vets were in the theatre that afternoon, Malcolm, who had already been at the hospital two years, and the boss.

An hour and a half later Cassie was lying on her back, hooked up to the anaesthetic machine and being prepared for surgery while I was scrubbing up. The operation is not difficult. First, I made an incision in the mid-line of the abdomen in the area where all the muscles attach. This is called the *linea alba*; the Latin term means 'white line', which is exactly what it looks like and you can achieve a relatively bloodless incision there. Immediately the bladder popped up into view. It was wrinkled and thickened, the typical appearance of a bladder that has been irritated by the foreign bodies – the stones. Another incision and there they were, looking rather beautiful, just like newly laid eggs in a nest. I removed them, then carefully stitched up the bladder wall using a material that would dissolve. All that remained was to repair the *linea alba* and the skin.

About three-quarters of an hour later, Cassie was coughing out her anaesthetic tube and blinking up at me.

'Well done,' Mary said.

'Well done to you,' I replied.

I was beside myself with joy. It had all gone so well. That night, before turning in, I popped into ward one to see my patient. At the time I had a flat above the hospital and this had become a regular routine, especially as I used to worry about some of the cases – a habit I have yet to drop. Cassie wagged her tail and rolled over to show off her stitches. A pat on her head and I was off to bed. I didn't go into the night staff's room otherwise I would have been swapping stories into the early hours – a favourite pastime.

The next day Cassie was apparently none the worse for her op and she was sent home after my boss had seen her on ward rounds. These days, we would analyse the type of stone we had removed and select a special commercial diet for her to prevent recurrence of the problem, but in the seventies we didn't have the array of treatment now available and she went home on antibiotics. She never looked back, however, and ten days later I was taking out her stitches and doubly pleased to see uneventful healing. Everyone was beaming. Me, Cassie – in her doggy kind of way – Mary, who had popped into the consulting room, and, of course, her devoted owners.

A couple of weeks later I got a postcard from County Cork. Cassie was with the Molloys and doing just fine. On their return there would be a bottle for me of something special from the Emerald Isle. This had to be the best of being a vet!

Cassie's bladder stones did not recur and she died in her sleep at the old age of sixteen. I was pleased that her owners had managed that trip to Ireland because a few months later Mr Molloy's father died peacefully. Today I still think of Cassie with a smile whenever I do a cystotomy – my first major op and a lesson in the joys of being a vet.

CHAPTER FIVE

The Ambulance Service

The ambulance service used to be based at the Harmsworth but a few years ago it was decided that it should be established elsewhere. There would be less strain on the switchboard, and less strain on me, too, as it would cease to be my responsibility.

The ambulance drivers work on a shift system so that there is twenty-four-hour cover, and their main role is to collect injured stray cats and rescue wildlife. They are controlled from the regional office, based in south London, which is where all RSPCA phone calls are routed except those to the hospital. The ambulance drivers work in tandem with the inspectors and, in theory, help to free up the inspectors to concentrate on their main role, investigating cruelty complaints. This does not always work and when things get busy the inspectors still do some rescues and collections. At times it is a stressful job and the drivers must be able to deal with the public under difficult circumstances in the same way as the inspectors. It is a much smaller operation than the human ambulance service, which causes problems at busy periods, for the service covers most of the area within the M25. The drivers are trained by the RSPCA, which involves spending time in the hospitals. The course attempts to cover all the many situations likely to be thrown at them. They need to be tough, resourceful and have lots of common sense, as you will see from Benji's case.

The day Benji decided to go for a walk on his own was a day his owner would never forget. Mrs Jenkins was nearly blind and lived on her own. Benji was the only thing that really mattered to her. Normally a friend or neighbour would come each day to take him out, and often Mrs Jenkins too, but that day the door was left open and Benji wandered off. Normally this wouldn't have been anything to worry about – he was a cautious little dog, knew the area well and pretty soon would have become worried at being on his own. None of these factors was relevant, though, because as soon as he arrived at the nearby park he was set upon by a pack of stray dogs. He was only the size of a Yorkshire terrier and offered no resistance. Most dogs will not carry on fighting when the other dog offers no resistance but these four continued to savage Benji until they were chased away by a group of boys. Benji staggered off, trying to get home, but after a few hundred yards he collapsed in the gutter, bleeding and semi-conscious. The boys had the presence of mind to ask local people to phone for a vet and the RSPCA was contacted first. By pure chance, one of only two ambulances on duty was not far away. The driver, Garry, arrived within minutes and made a quick assessment of the situation.

Benji was obviously very shocked and needed to be transported to hospital – and fast. But first the bleeding must be stopped. Garry put a pressure bandage on the main wound on Benji's chest, checked for any broken bones, then placed a blanket on the ground. Gently he rolled the badly injured dog onto the blanket, then with the help of one of the boys, lifted him into the back of the ambulance. This is the standard way of getting an injured dog into a car or ambulance and many animals' lives would be saved if rescuers did this rather than phoning round to try to get a vet out to the scene. Vets are usually either consulting or operating, and it is far quicker to get the dog into the hospital.

Local people around at the time recognised Benji, and knew his owner, but there was no time to contact her, so the boys were dispatched to Mrs Jenkins to let her know what had happened and to give her the hospital telephone number. In fact, Mrs Jenkins phoned even before the ambulance had arrived, but the nurse promised that we would call her back as soon as we had any news. It must have been a harrowing time for her, but we, too, were in for some worrying hours.

At the hospital I was waiting with the duty theatre nurse. We had been alerted by the ambulance radio that Benji was coming in and that he was very poorly. Garry's action had undoubtedly saved him from dying there and then, but the dog was not yet out of danger. When he reached us, Benji was suffering from severe shock. His mucous membranes were ashen grey, his pulse was hardly discernible, and although he was conscious he wasn't really with it. Immediately Benji came in I set up a drip fluid to counteract the shock: it wasn't easy because his blood pressure was low and I had trouble finding a vein. At this stage I felt that there was a high risk of losing him. I decided to use a special solution to expand blood volume, followed by Hartmann's, a balanced electrolyte solution, which I pumped into Benji as fast as possible along with steroids, which help in shock, and painkillers. All this was filmed during the first series, and as the performance went out live, the viewing public had no idea whether or not he would survive. Like millions of others, I could only hope.

Once the drip was set up it was over to the nurses for intensive care. Benji was checked constantly for the next twenty-four hours as we monitored his response to the treatment for shock. One test we use is to press the lining of a lip until it blanches, then time how quickly the colour comes back after removing the finger. This is called the capillary refill time and in a normal dog should happen almost instantaneously. In Benji's case it took four seconds – which is bad. Four hours later there was a distinct improvement: it had gone up to two seconds and his colour was pinker. He was going to make it – at least as far as getting over the shock was concerned.

Over ward rounds the next day I pondered what to do next for Benji. It was time to assess his wounds and investigate him in a little more depth. Bairbre O'Malley did this, with Benji under full general anaesthesia. She found the penetrating wound to his chest, which had nearly cost Benji his life, and another couple of deep wounds in his abdomen. She stitched them up and set up another drip for the next twenty-four hours. Within a day we saw the first wag of his tail and Benji was soon yelling for his food. But it was a week before I felt confident enough to let him go home, where he was duly delivered by another ambulance driver.

The welcome he got brought a tear to everyone's eyes. Mrs Jenkins was sitting on her settee and Benji bounded in, to smother her with licks. He went on to make a complete recovery and Mrs Jenkins now has a child gate in place to prevent him wandering off again. So often it takes an accident to happen before we think of the means to prevent it.

The ambulance drivers are always on the go, especially in the summer. They often have to bring in swans for first aid and assessment. Most of these patients are transferred to the swan sanctuary in Egham where they have built up expertise in dealing with them and have space and the facilities we lack.

Swans are beautiful and it is always distressing to see them ill. I had to examine a particularly fine specimen one hot summer's afternoon. He had been seen to be listless on the lake in one of the local parks and was not feeding. A member of the public phoned the office and Kieran, the driver, easily caught the bird. The most noticeable thing about the swan was his extreme lethargy: he could not hold up his neck, which kept flopping onto his breast. I gave some fluids by stomach tube and then phoned our wildlife hospital for advice. The veterinary manager there, Ian Robinson, listened to my account of the swan's symptoms and said that he probably had botulism. Jeremy had seen one with similar symptoms earlier, which had gone to the swan sanctuary.

Botulism is a bacterial disease caused by a germ called *clostridium botulinum*, which is similar to the one that causes tetanus. Ian told me that it wasn't unusual to see cases in the heat of summer, particularly when it had been raining after a drought. Water levels in lakes may have dropped and risen with the rain. In the shallow parts of the lake rotting vegetation and food make an ideal substrate for the botulism agent. The swan's almost paralysed neck was a typical symptom. I was told that survival or otherwise would depend on the amount of the botulinus toxin that had been ingested. The treatment should consist of fluids, and supportive nursing. Further treatment would be best carried out at the sanctuary and Kieran made arrangements with the office to take the swan over there. He would be carried in a special jacket that fitted neatly round her body leaving the neck and head free. I kept my fingers crossed that he would survive and that in due course a driver would be able to return him to his mate. One of the most endearing characteristics of swans is that they mate for life.

Although the drivers never know what they will pick up next, the main part of their work involves cats. Cats are curious animals and when they are young this often gets them into mischief. Some cats, and our Penny was one, adore climbing trees. Penny used to chase squirrels and birds, always unsuccessfully, but in the process she became an expert tree-climber. Fortunately the trees in our garden are many-branched and it was easy for her to get up and down. Plod, though, could not be described as a natural athlete. He hadn't been named Plod for nothing: from birth he had always seemed slower than his litter mates. Unusually for a kitten he had shown little interest in going outside and if he did it was only for a few minutes. He was a home-lover and didn't relish the cold. In the spring, though, when it began to get warmer he ventured out a bit more. His owners had no idea why he took it into his head to climb a large sycamore outside his house and they didn't think much of it at first. Perhaps it had something to do with a couple of aggressive toms, which regarded Plod's garden as their territory. Some cat wailing had been going on and soon after that Plod was seen half-way up the tree. Most tree-climbing cats will come down, especially when they are hungry, but Plod was an exception. At ten o'clock that night his worried owners called the RSPCA, and Kieran was dispatched to see what could be done.

Plod was quite high up and resting on a branch. If anything, he seemed to be enjoying all the attention. Climbing the tree without a ladder was out of the question so the problem was shelved until the next morning. There was enough light from street lamps for

Plod to see his way down if he decided to end his vigil.

The next morning Plod was getting worried. Far from attempting to come down he had decided, for reasons best known to himself, to climb even higher. He had now been up the tree for thirty-six hours and would have to be brought down if he refused to co-operate. A big bowl of best-quality cat food was placed at the bottom of the tree and everybody left the scene. Within five minutes one of the resident toms had arrived and scoffed the lot.

Kieran decided to call out the fire brigade. The fire brigade and the RSPCA often get together for a dual effort, but the brigade won't turn out until an assessment of the situation has been made by the RSPCA. Twenty minutes later Plod was in the arms of a fire-fighter, who had gone up a huge ladder and plucked him from a thin branch near the top of the tree. Plod had a placid nature so he hadn't needed to use a grasper, a kind of snare used temporarily to restrain frightened or vicious cats. Once home, the cat ate and then slept for twenty-four hours.

Rescuing animals from high in trees is potentially dangerous so don't try it yourself. It's always best left to people with experience and the necessary equipment, backed up by the RSPCA.

Plod had apparently learned his lesson: he wouldn't go out for several months and then restricted himself to his back garden where there weren't any trees. He learned eventually to use a magnet-controlled cat flap and could bolt home in the event of any trouble.

Another situation that the drivers are often called in to resolve is when cats are trapped in buildings, garages or sheds. This is worrying to their owners because the cat simply disappears. Usually if it is trapped it will be somewhere not far away and if you lose a cat it is worthwhile to ask everyone in your road to check any outbuildings. My wife had to do this once when Penny disappeared for twenty-four hours. It turned out that she had investigated someone's kitchen and when the owner returned she hid under a unit. When she was discovered, she refused to come out, despite much pleading and tempting, and, watched rather anxiously by our neighbour, I had to dismantle the unit before grabbing her unceremoniously. Fortunately I was able to put it back together again but DIY is not my forte.

The ambulance service also deals with birds and other animals stranded behind gas fires or up chimneys. This happens so regularly that the standard procedures manual, which all hospital employees work through during their training, carries instructions on how to deal with it. An assessment is made and if the animal cannot be released by the ambulance driver, the gas board and/or the fire brigade are summoned. If a bird is fluttering about behind a gas fire it can be caught only by dismantling the appliance, a matter for the gas-board experts. Cats who decide to crawl up a chimney may either get stuck or refuse to come down. Last year a young cat went exploring up a chimney only to get stuck at the top. After its owners and the RSPCA had spent a few fruitless days trying to get it down, the fire brigade had to dismantle the chimney stack before they could rescue its bewildered and hungry occupant.

I experienced something similar when I homed a

kitten to a friend called Sue. She was desperate for a ginger cat and the kitten was one of four who had been dumped in a rubbish chute in a plastic bag. Their plaintive mewing had been heard and the RSPCA had been called. A few days later, a ginger tom was wending his way to a life of opulence in a smart house complete with its own housekeeper. 'Any problems, just give me a ring,' I had said airily, as the kitten was put in a box.

I couldn't believe it when I got a phone call half an hour later. The kitten had leapt out of the box and disappeared up a disused chimney. There had been no sign of him since.

'Don't worry,' I said, with greater conviction than I felt. 'I expect he'll come down when he's hungry. What is it now? Ten o'clock. Give me a call at five if he's still there.' At two minutes past five my friend was on the line. The kitten was still up the chimney, as evidenced by occasional flurries of soot that fell into the fireplace.

'I'll pop in on the way home,' I said, 'and see what can be done.' I made a mental note of which drivers were on duty in case I needed their expertise – I didn't want to be the one to call out the fire brigade!

At six o'clock I was surveying the situation. I clambered behind the fire and looked up the chimney with a torch. Two anxious feline eyes peered back at me. Ginger had reached a ledge about seven feet up and could probably climb higher if he was frightened. Sue and I had a cup of tea while we thought about what to do.

'Have you tried tempting him down with food?' I

With my dog Barney outside the Harmsworth
(© Ken McKay/RSPCA)

The veterinary team: (left to right) Stan, Bairbre, Jeremy, me,

Rolf, Andrea, Gabriel, Helen holding
her dog Stumpy (© BBC)

Barney, who I rescued as a puppy.

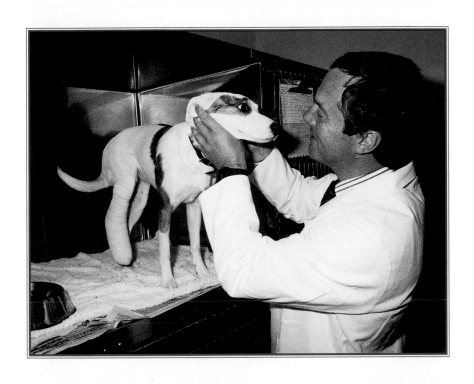

Lisa Kopper with a recovered Duchess -
now called Dolly
(© Caroline Mardon)

Gordon with Snowy as she is today (© Caroline Mardon)

When she was brought in to the hospital it was
impossible to tell what breed she was
(© RSPCA)

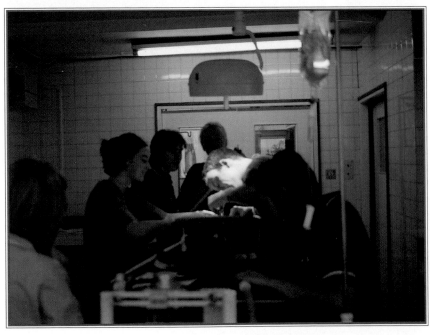

Preparing an anaesthetic (© Geoff Langan/RSPCA)

(Top right) In the prep room, preparing a cat with
a ruptured diaphram for surgery (© David Grant)

(Bottom left) The emergency operation in progress,
with four nurses, a student vet and Gabriel
operating (© David Grant)

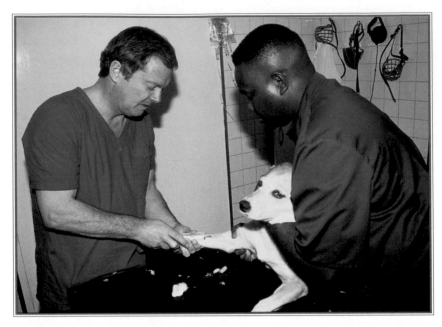

Adminstering an anaesthetic (© Ken McKay/RSPCA)

Stan in operating theatre 2 with nurse Claire (© David Grant)

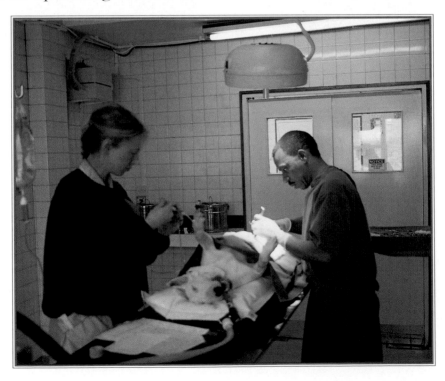

Taking an X-ray of an anaesthetised cat
(© Geoff Langan/RSPCA)

Explaining an X-ray to Rolf -
this one shows a dog with a slipped disc
(© Link Photography/RSPCA)

On night duty,
outside the
hospital with
ambulance
driver
Kieran Graham
(© Tim
Sambrook/
RSPCA)

asked.

'Yes, but he seems too frightened to bother.'

I looked at the rather unappetising mash in the saucer. 'Have you got anything more exciting?' I wondered, and a tin of pilchards appeared. Sue put a saucer on the hearth and we waited for the aroma of pilchards to take effect. Ten seconds later Ginger landed in a great cloud of soot and attacked his dish. I tried to grab him but he shot off round the room across the – horrors – beige and expensive-looking carpet, leaving an amazing trail of sooty paw prints. From there he bounded on to the equally opulent sofa. One more frantic, and failed, attempt to catch him propelled him into the bathroom. I slammed the door shut.

'Leave him there to calm down,' I said, as I pushed in what was left of the pilchards.

'And while he's there we might as well give him a bath. He certainly needs it!'

I surveyed the mess that had once been a lovely, elegant drawing room, wondering whether this friendship was doomed. But Sue was so relieved that her new pet was safe that she didn't seem to mind the chaos. But we found worse when we entered the bathroom. The décor, including the carpets, was white – or, at least, it had been. Now it was a patchy grey and black. The cause of the mayhem had fallen into an exhausted sleep on the deep-pile carpet near the washbasin, which I filled with lukewarm water. I bathed the kitten gently, in his new owner's expensive soap, which quickly brought out his natural beautiful colours. With a full tummy, clean and warm, he went back to sleep in his newly acquired bed while we blocked off the remaining chimneys with bits of wood. It was some time before I homed another kitten...

On one occasion the ambulance service had been alerted to a possible trapped cat in a deserted house. According to the neighbours, nobody had been seen in the house for nearly three weeks and a tabby cat, which was often in the gardens, had not been seen either. Loud miaowing had been heard from within the house over the last three days. This was a job for the ambulance service and the inspector. The cat would need to be rescued, transported to the hospital, given treatment and, most importantly, careful feeding. In the meantime the inspector would try to catch whoever had abandoned it.

Rescuing the cat was quite a business. To get access the police had to assist with breaking into the house. They also had to be present in case someone had died. It took about five minutes to kick in the door. A rapid search of the house didn't locate the cat at first, but there was plenty of evidence of its presence – the house was in a bit of a mess. There was no evidence of any food but a tap was dripping in the kitchen, which would have kept the animal alive.

Suddenly Garry, the ambulance driver, caught sight of a frightened face peering from under a bed. It took half an hour to catch the cat as it dashed from one room to another, pursued by Garry. Finally it was cornered in the kitchen and Garry grabbed it with the aid of a pair of gloves. The cat was exhausted and was gently put into a basket to calm down and be taken to hospital. Next the house was checked: it showed no sign of habitation, although there were lots of letters on the front door mat, which might help the police to trace – and prosecute – the previous occupants.

When we examined the cat at the Harmsworth we discovered that he was an entire male and very thin. He weighed only 2 kilos. Cats and dogs differ from humans in that they can survive starvation quite well, providing that they have access to water. They usually recover surprisingly quickly. Tom, as he was named, doubled his weight in just a few weeks and was soon found a home. His previous owners were never traced.

Perhaps surprisingly an ambulance driver rescues a large number of injured pigeons. There are, of course, millions in London, and they become ill or injured just like any other animal. Many are run over when they misjudge the speed at which a car is travelling and fail to get out of the way at the last minute. Many break legs or wings in flying accidents and others just become sick – a reflection of poor hygiene and overcrowding. Much of the work involved with these birds is to prevent suffering, and humane destruction is often necessary. If you find an injured bird, remember it should be restrained. The best thing to do is to place a box over it until the ambulance arrives. Otherwise experience has shown that the bird, injured or not, will have flown by the time help is at hand.

We also see numerous kestrels, crows, blackbirds and even some quite rare birds. Most have been rescued either with injuries or as a result of exhaustion, following adverse weather conditions. They have included nightjars, woodpeckers, cormorants, grebes, sparrowhawks and many others – over forty different species in all. Many need to be treated and rehabilitated by bird specialists and the drivers may find themselves taking the patient to an RSPCA wildlife hospital. The one nearest the Harmsworth is in north Norfolk. Our nurses occasionally change places with their counterparts at this hospital and there couldn't be a greater contrast in the work and environment. They learn how to encourage hedgehogs to unroll and how to handle birds correctly and sometimes deal with more complicated problems, such as cleaning severely oiled birds.

To a certain extent I envy my wildlife colleagues their environment, but to acquire their knowledge would be a huge undertaking so I am set to stay at the Harmsworth. Trips to the wildlife hospital are popular with all of the staff and I have been there several times. I have never heard a driver complain about a journey with wildlife to Norfolk!

Chapter Six

Environmental Hazards

At the Harmsworth we also run an outpatient clinic at which we encounter virtually all the clinical conditions under the sun. It's a marvellous place to get experience and it brings home to both us and pet owners how easy it is for an animal to injure itself in its own environment.

One Wednesday morning when we were filming, I was examining the appropriately named Jack – a Jack Russell terrier. At first sight there was nothing much the matter with him. In fact many people wouldn't have bothered to bring him in for examination although later, as things got worse, they would have had to. Jack had been rubbing his nose and there was now a bald patch on the side. He was a sprightly fifteen-year-old showing little sign of ageing, and the same could be said of his owners, Mr and Mrs James, a retired couple. They knew their dog, and a bald patch on the side of his nose didn't seem right.

Jack Russells are active, brave little dogs and this one didn't seem to mind me pulling his nose about – in fact, he took the stance that many of his breed do, which was to act as if I wasn't there. He didn't look at me or acknowledge my presence in any way. I examined the bald patch and noticed a sharp line of demarcation between abnormal and normal skin. I had seen this kind of thing before and alarm bells sounded. If this was what I thought it was, we would have to nip it in the bud or things would get a lot worse.

'Do you have any hedgehogs in your garden?' I asked.

Mr James looked puzzled. 'Well, as a matter of fact we have,' he replied.

'And does Jack like to roll them like footballs?' Apparently he did. I felt I was near to a diagnosis. Jack Russells are the footballers of the canine world and a rolled-up hedgehog will do if they come across one. I know of few other dogs foolish enough to attempt this. Apart from getting a sore nose, they run the risk of hedgehog ringworm: the fungal spores are inoculated by the hedgehog's prickles into the injured skin. This, I thought, was almost certainly Jack's problem, but I had to prove it. I took samples of hair from the little dog's nose and put them in a special medium for growing fungi.

Although the word ringworm is familiar enough, many people don't appreciate that it is a fungal infection. Athlete's foot is a well-known example of the same kind of thing. The medium used for the first part of the diagnosis turns red if ringworm is present and in this case it had turned red quickly, within four days. I was pleased: I normally allow up to fourteen days. If the medium hasn't changed colour by then the test is considered negative. I immediately started treatment for Jack with griseofulvin, a drug specifically for fungal infections.

Meanwhile I recultured the positive test on to another medium to see if I could identify the fungus as having come from a hedgehog. Hedgehog fungus is called *Trichophyton erinacei* and, sure enough, after a week the characteristic white colony with yellow underside was there to see. That was very satisfying. And it was even better to see at his first check-up that Jack was making rapid progress. We had caught it in time and saved him months of discomfort. I have seen other dogs afflicted with the same disease in which the fungus had spread rapidly from the nose to cover almost the entire body. When these advanced cases are treated it can take many months before any improvement is seen.

One fortunate thing about hedgehog ringworm is that dogs don't pass it on easily to humans, and Jack's owners were clear of it. In fact, of all the types of ringworm that dogs can get this is one of the less common, and in most cases we see in dogs we find that they have caught it from a cat. Ringworm is much more common in cats than in dogs.

The next day we saw a poodle, Pepsi, with a complaint we encounter often in late July and August. I had three similar cases on that day. At least it wasn't three Caesareans or three gastric torsions. Pepsi's problem was a grass seed.

Grass seeds are a real problem in some dogs because they lodge in awkward places. Pepsi's was stuck in his paw. He simply wouldn't leave it alone and wouldn't let his owner look at it. The paw was obviously painful, as he tried to bite me when I touched it. I tied up his mouth with a piece of bandage and had another go. There between the pads was the tell-tale swelling and infection that every vet knows is associated with a grass seed, especially so in the height of summer. They are very sharp and penetrate the skin easily. Once in they don't come out easily, due to their barbs which point backwards. In short they have to be pulled out. For the most part this means a general anaesthetic.

Pepsi hadn't eaten that day so almost immediately I gave him a GA. A quick incision and there it was, a little way up in the paw. I removed it and kept it to show the owners, an elderly retired couple. Within a week, with the help of some antibiotics, the paw would heal perfectly. Pepsi was already coming round as Nicky the nurse secured the bandage. In some parts of the south of France and also in Spain the word for grass seed is *espiga*, and I know of one vet who sees so many cases that he calls his practice the Espiga Veterinary Clinic.

My next grass seed was in a spaniel's ear, another

common site. Not too difficult to make the diagnosis – in fact, the owner had already made it. Poor Toby's head was on one side, and he was scratching furiously at his ear, crying at the same time. His owner added that it had come on after his morning walk – through a field. I gave Toby a general anaesthetic and found the seed right beside the ear drum. I had it out in two seconds using the special crocodile forceps specially designed for the purpose. A quick look in the other ear revealed another on its way down. When I was first qualified I learned from one of my bosses always to look in both ears and also the animal's paws. It's a little embarrassing to send the poor dog home only to be presented with it again the next day showing the same symptoms.

The third case that morning was unusual. An old tom cat was brought in with a severely inflamed eye, which was discharging pus. He could hardly open it and he had been like this for about a week. The owner had been bathing the eye in weak tea, an old-fashioned remedy which I don't recommend. If your pet suffers from eye trouble, don't try to treat it yourself: you risk damaging the eye permanently. I couldn't see immediately what was causing the cat's discomfort so I instilled a little opthaine, a local anaesthetic, into the eye, and within a minute it was wide open.

In the corner of the upper eyelid I could see the stalk of a grass seed. A gentle tug and it was out. I put in some drops of a stain called fluorescein, which fills in any ulcers on the cornea making them visible. The seed had indeed left an ulcer, and the cat needed an intensive course of antibiotics but I was confident that it's sight would be saved.

Poisoning, another environmental hazard, always seems to happen out of hours, especially late at night, and often involves young animals. Older ones are too wise to mess about with strange substances. Puppies, in particular, are inclined to eat whatever they find and need a constant eye kept on them – just like children. Keep all medicines out of reach!

The little nine-week-old Labrador puppy, Robby, rushed in at 10 p.m. one Saturday night, didn't seem to be in any danger. He bounced around the surgery floor looking very pleased with himself. His owner, Mrs Glennie, was worried that he had eaten two months' supply of her contraceptive pill! She had been out for a quick meal and had come home to find the contents of one of her drawers strewn all over the bedroom and various items of furniture chewed up. Among the mess she found the packets of pills with the contents gone. I looked up the name of the pill and it seemed that the amount of oestrogen was low even with two months' supply. However, there is a theoretical danger of bone-marrow suppression with oestrogenic hormones so I telephoned the National Poisons Unit for advice. Someone reassured me quickly that the puppy was unlikely to become ill but that he should be given liquid paraffin to help push out the tin foil. They had had several calls on the same subject in the last month .

But Mrs Glennie was really worried and wanted to be absolutely sure. 'Couldn't you make him vomit?' she asked. I didn't think that was necessary or would be of much use. Most chewing episodes occur as soon as the owner leaves the house so Robby might have eaten the pills at least three hours ago: by now they would be in the intestines and would not come up with any vomit. I told Mrs Glennie that if Robby showed any sign of illness in the next day or so, we would take a blood sample, and that would reveal whether there was any problem but I didn't anticipate any trouble.

The next afternoon Robby was back. Mrs Glennie's five-year-old son had been playing with marbles, Robby had just pounced on one and swallowed it. I examined his tummy and straightaway I could feel a round object. Now it would be worth trying to make him sick. I put some washing-soda crystals on his tongue and held his mouth shut for a minute or so. Vets often use this technique to induce vomiting and it works in most cases, but don't try it yourself without asking a vet first: in some circumstances if you make a dog vomit the situation worsens.

An anxious expression came over Robby's little face and five minutes later he brought up his midday meal. With a clunk the marble appeared – much to everybody's relief, because we did not want to open up such a young dog.

Poor Mrs Glennie was rather embarrassed that she had had to rush her puppy in to us twice within twenty-four hours, especially as she had also had to visit the local casualty unit with her little boy, who had fallen over and broken his arm. I knew just how she felt. 'Don't worry,' I said, 'I've had several trips up there myself recently and I was thinking that the doctors would be marking me down as an excessively anxious parent. But when I looked around I saw half a dozen kids who'd all had some sort of mishap. Several of them were there for the second or third time. You need eyes in the back of your head with dogs and children!'

I didn't tell her that when I had been in Casualty I'd asked one of the older ladies waiting there when I could hope for an end to my children's accident phase, and her forty-year-old son walked out: he had been visiting her and cut himself slicing bread! Instead, I glanced down at Robby: I had a feeling that it might not be the last we saw of him either. 'Keep an eye on him at all times if you can,' I said to his owner. 'Before you go out have a look round and try to think what he could get up to and what he could chew, especially your favourite pieces of furniture.'

I couldn't believe my eyes when I saw him a month later. Mrs Glennie had gone out to do the shopping and left Robby in the kitchen. He had knocked over the rubbish bin and eaten half its contents but, worse still, had got his nose and tongue stuck in a half-open baked-beans tin. He looked very comical at first, but the smile was soon wiped off my face. Robby's tongue was trapped between the lid and the side of the tin and getting it out was going to be tricky. If he panicked there was a real danger it would be cut it very badly. There was no time to lose. I gave him an anaesthetic there and then on the consulting table, while Mrs Glennie held and calmed him. It was an awkward job. In the end, I got a tin opener and managed to get the lid right off, and Robby's tongue was free. Ten minutes later he was conscious, wagging his tail and having forgotten, no doubt, what the hue and cry was all about. Since then he has been on a tight rein and accident free – thank goodness!

The chewing phase normally lasts only a few months. Most dogs grow out of it as they become adults and can then be left alone safely. Those few months can be a pain, though, and I remembered the antics Barney used to get up to at that age,

Poisons, though, are a far bigger worry for the pet owner and the vet. Some are well recognised and not difficult to diagnose – Warfarin in rat poison, for example, which causes haemorrhage and severe anaemia. Most vets will have dealt with this at some time. Others are less common and more likely to be seen in inner-city areas. Buster was a one-year-old Staffordshire bull terrier who, unusually, came in early at ten one morning. He was in a state of apparent confusion, standing and walking with difficulty. His eyes were staring and he seemed quite agitated. Noise startled him and at first I thought he might be suffering from some form of epilepsy. His owner could not throw any light on what might have happened. He said he had been to an all night party and had come home first thing in the morning to let Buster out and found him in this semi-collapsed state.

I took the dog in for observation and tests. As he walked with the nurse he became even more agitated and kept falling over. We gave him a sedative into the vein and put up a drip. At the same time I took some blood for testing. Perhaps that way I'd get a diagnosis.

'I wonder if he's eaten something?' I thought aloud.

Jill, the nurse, said, 'It looks like hash to me.'

'Have you seen something like this before?' I asked. She said she had.

'But his owner says he hasn't eaten anything!'

Jill smiled and asked if I would like her to talk to Jim. He had been very upset and was still in the hospital – he wanted to wait and see how Buster got on. Five minutes later Jill was back. 'He says Buster's probably eaten some cannabis.'

I phoned the Poisons Unit straight away and was given some useful advice. I had been right to put Buster on a drip, he would need sedating, and should be given some activated charcoal via a stomach tube. Recovery should occur within twenty-four hours. The next morning on my ward rounds I could hear Buster from half-way up the corridor: he was letting out that peculiar wail, rather like a baby, that is so characteristic of Staffordshire bull terriers. There were no signs of any tremors.

An hour later Jim was back to take him home, looking so sheepish and worried that I felt it was unlikely to happen again. Apparently the drug had been left near some chocolates and Buster had decided he might as well eat that too. He had simply been left too long on his own – a point I hammered home to Jim. I hoped that the experience had taught him a lesson, and, certainly, I've never seen a similar case happen twice to the same animal.

But not all poisonings are so easily resolved. A young puppy was brought in recently after he had eaten a load of paracetamol tablets. The owners noticed the chewed-up empty pill bottle but couldn't be sure how many tablets the puppy had eaten or when. It was too late to wash out his stomach – gastric lavage – as he was already ill. He had started to vomit and his whole body was tinged yellow, most obviously around the mouth and in the whites of the eyes, which may indicate massive liver damage.

As the nurses set up a drip I said to his owners, a couple who looked no older than teenagers although they had a young baby with them, that I didn't expect the puppy to recover. They weren't going to give in without a fight, though, and begged us to try. Jeremy had already been on to the Poisons Unit and had been given the name of an antidote drug, which he went up to the local general hospital to collect. We started giving this into the drip daily and kept going with the fluids, antibiotics and large doses of B vitamins. The puppy was young and the liver has amazing powers of rejuvenation, if it hasn't been totally destroyed.

We battled on for a week without any obvious sign that the puppy was getting better. However when we compared the results of his first blood tests with the latest ones he was showing some improvement. We decided to push on. Gradually, over the next fortnight, he made progress and started to take food for himself and keep it down. He was woefully thin and I was worried that if he picked up anything else it would finish him off. He was sent home, with a prayer, to be fed little and often. Two weeks on, it was obvious he was going to pull through. I was amazed and delighted to see the poor little object that I had fully expected to die bounding with the enthusiasm for life that makes puppies so special.

All poisoning is potentially preventable, and one of the most heartrending letters I received during the transmission of *Animal Hospital* was from a boy of eight, whose cat had died after drinking antifreeze. Apparently it tastes sweet and some cats will lick it if any is spilt. But it is very toxic to the kidneys and the boy's cat had died in this way. He wanted me to announce the danger on television to make sure that it didn't happen to anyone else's cat. Unfortunately we can't give out messages like this within the format of the programme. For a start, they sound forced and unnatural and if you are constantly sending out messages soap-box style the programme would quickly become boring and people would stop watching. There are lots of animal-welfare messages that I would love to get over to everyone about neutering, vaccination, identification of pets and so on, but they come across best shown as a result of a case arriving at the hospital, when the animal itself would very visibly, and compellingly, make the point.

CHAPTER SEVEN

Pets and their Owners

When I was eleven, I decided I was going to be a vet. It didn't occur to me that I would do anything else. At that age I loved animals, as most children do, and I wanted to make them better when they were ill. Far nicer, I thought, than having to deal with people all day as a doctor. The fact that animals have owners didn't occur to me! And owners usually form a bond with their pets just as strong in its way as that between parents and their children. All vets have to be able to relate to and like other people or their lives would be miserable. Many of my vet friends enjoy consulting because after a while many of their clients become friends, they get to know the whole family, and a relationship builds up between them similar to that between the GP and his or her patients.

There is no specific guidance at veterinary college on dealing with the public at a professional level, although sometimes students do a little consulting under supervision. By the time I qualified, most of my 'seeing practice', which is the term used to describe student time with qualified vets, had been spent in farm work and I had had little contact with people and their pets. I had to learn as I went along after qualification, and the owners were quick to spot any indecision on my part. I also had to learn to try to understand the relationship an owner had with their pet, which influences how far they are be prepared to go in any investigation and treatment.

By and large people were very kind and after a year or so my confidence soared, although not before I had faced many anxieties. In my first year I had an almost permanent frown of concentration, and there was little time for anything else in my life. I was given a lot of help by experienced colleagues – something I have never forgotten.

Even now, though, after so many years of practice, I don't often have to examine an owned ferret. Ferret-keeping is a specialist hobby and we don't have much to do with them. However, ferrets turn up regularly as strays and finding a home for them is a real problem. They're a bit smelly, to put it mildly, and need a lot of training. This is why I was examining Whisky. His owner had a strange tale to tell, which he recounted to *Animal Hospital*'s viewers. As the consultation wore on, I began to regret that we were being filmed...

Mr Saunders was a keen fisherman and Whisky had turned up in his life one day while he was out with his rods. The ferret had suddenly darted out of the bushes at the side of the river and come up to him. Mr Saunders had picked him up and taken him home. He and Whisky had bonded immediately, as so often happens between owner and pet, and Whisky became part of the family. Ferrets, like many other animals, know when they are on to a good thing. Whisky had found someone to feed and care for him – what more could he ask for?

But Whisky was an adolescent male ferret and it wasn't long before a power struggle developed between him and Mr Saunders as to who was boss. Whisky had taken to nipping his owner whenever it took his fancy, which was whenever he was annoyed. Mr Saunders had brought him along for a check-up and advice.

Ferrets are not my strong point but I reckoned that what we had here was a problem that could be treated only with some kind of training programme. Now this is easy if it's a dog you're dealing with, but ferret training programmes are thin on the ground. So I had to work from basic principles. Tentatively I got Whisky out of his box. Ferrets are difficult to handle so I was cautious but he didn't bite me and my confidence grew. I told Mr Saunders that most animals naturally belong to a pack and expect there to be a leader, a boss. In the case of pets, dogs, for example, this should be the owner and ferrets were no different. I put Whisky on his back, which made me dominant. He remained submissive and motionless. I suggested that to make things easier castration might be the answer. Testosterone, the male sex hormone, is the major cause of aggression in animals (some would argue that it is the cause of most of the world's problems) and castration is effective in reducing aggression not only towards the owner but to other animals.

Mr Saunders would have none of it. It is only men who ever resist the concept of castration and Mr Saunders, who I liked, belonged to this category. So did Whisky: for as soon as I mentioned castration he wriggled out of my grip and inflicted a warning bite on my finger. Then he tried to disappear down my trousers, to my alarm but to the huge amusement of everyone else. Then I lost it. I grabbed Whisky to stop him disappearing and he sank his teeth into my thumb. The pain was excruciating. Bleeding profusely I needed help to detach him, and eventually we got him back into his box. 'There you are,' I said, with a hint of triumph but perhaps also a desire for revenge. 'Get him castrated as soon as possible!' I was trying to stay serious but then I spotted Rolf shaking with laughter and saw the funny side. Serves me right for bragging about being dominant.

Some months later I saw Mr Saunders with his dog and the conversation inevitably worked round to Whisky. He had not been castrated but he had been taught who was boss. Now when Mr Saunders goes fishing Whisky sits on his head under his hat, causing consternation to fellow fishermen whenever he pops out to see what's going on. So, everything has turned out very well – but I still maintain that castration would make him a better pet although I'm not going to push it for the sake of my thumb!

Surprisingly often, though, relationships between pets and their owners can go wrong when the pet, more often than not a dog, assumes a dominant role over one or more members of the family. Tyson's dominance over his owners was evident. He had little to do with them, preferring to spend much of his time in his favourite resting places, a chair in front of the fire or the owners' bed. Mr Bailey was out a lot and occasionally worked away from home while Mrs Bailey stayed at home to look after the two children, aged four and six.

Although he was only a medium-sized dog, Tyson was described as having a temper and wouldn't obey Mrs Bailey. He took notice of her husband, but usually with bad grace growling at the simplest command. Things had come to a head when he had threatened the youngest child, who had tried to stroke him. Before that he had snapped at Mrs Bailey when she had tried to get him off her bed and she had backed down.

It was obvious that Tyson regarded himself as the head of the household. He had no respect for Mrs Bailey or the children and routinely did not obey their commands. His owners had reinforced this behaviour over the last year, including Mr Bailey, by backing down when they were involved in a confrontation, particularly over Tyson getting off the bed or a chair. Virtually all interactions were generated by the dog: if he wanted to go for a walk he would find his lead, bring it to the owners and bark. They had always thought this amusing and clever, and had rewarded him with a pat and, of course, a walk. If he wanted to go out to relieve himself, he would stand and whine by the door. When he felt hungry, he would stand by his bowl and bark until he was fed. Otherwise he would spend his days as he pleased, and most of the time his presence wasn't obvious. He growled at visitors so that several had been put off coming, and there had been the worrying escalation of threatening behaviour to the owners.

The owners loved Tyson, regarded him as one of the family and, by their own admission, had spoiled him 'rotten'. They made no attempt to discipline him for bad behaviour. Once or twice Mr Bailey admitted to having shouted at the dog and hit him with a rolled-up newspaper when Tyson had growled at him, but this had been only partially successful. It seemed that Tyson was forever trying it on.

They had come to the hospital to see if tranquillisers would help: they were getting desperate and were now considering the extreme solution of having him put down. But tranquillisers are never the answer with dogs and their nervous problems, except as a short-term measure, on Bonfire Night for example, and I never prescribe them for any other reason.

I explained to the Baileys that Tyson had gradually become dominant in the household and was now challenging the man of the house for total control. The only way to resolve this was by a training programme to reverse the dominant role that the dog had assumed. This would need a lot of hard work and time. My first suggestion was that both owners attend training classes with a local police-dog handler, who would teach them to apply basic commands such as sit, stay, come, etc., and begin the process of taking control from Tyson. The dog should also be castrated to reduce his aggression. He must never be left alone with the children, who were told that they must not touch him. He was to be excluded from the bedroom and not allowed on any chairs – initially the Baileys had to put objects on them to keep him off. He was to be ignored when he requested food or a walk, and when he pawed them for attention, they were not to react. Only when he was quiet would food be offered or would he be taken out. Any submissive behaviour, like sitting when he was told to, should be rewarded with a titbit.

At first it was difficult and Tyson barked incessantly, particularly when he was hungry, and he went through a phase of confusion, alternating between barking and whining. But after a few weeks the Baileys began to see an improvement: Tyson accepted the new ground rules, began to behave himself and stopped growling. The children were told to avoid him but he even became calmer towards them. The training had worked and it was pleasing that this had been achieved without threats, shouting or violence. After Tyson was castrated he became even easier to manage and some six months after the initial consultation, when euthanasia had been a real possibility, he had been transformed into a much more pleasant, trustworthy family pet.

Dogs are naturally pack animals and expect either to be dominated or to be dominant themselves. It is inevitably easier to own a dog if it is submissive to all members of the family. This can usually be achieved easily by simply being consistently in control, from the moment the dog is brought home and not deviating from this. Dominance is not achieved by frightening your pet but by disciplining him calmly – and not allowing him to call the shots!

The most extreme example of dominance aggression that I have seen recently was that of another male dog that had moved itself into the owners' bedroom, sleeping on their bed and not allowing them into the room – the whole family had been reduced to sleeping on the landing of their flat. The teenage son had tried to break the dog's dominance by challenging him, but had been bitten in the face for his pains. Not surprisingly, he had backed down, reinforcing the dog's dominance. When things have gone as far as this, the owners usually request that the dog be put down.

Bringing up a dog is a bit like bringing up a child, a lot of hard work and frustrating at times. Get it right, and you'll have a lot of pleasure from your pet. Get it wrong, and the animal becomes a source of unhappiness. Sorting out behavioural problems can be time-consuming, and most vets refer complicated cases to a behavioural consultant who can spend an hour or two with the owner. Sometimes this happens at the owner's house, where the whole family interaction can be studied. This is expensive, though, so in a case that hasn't gone too far, we give common-sense advice such as Tyson's owners received. I am always on the look-out for unacceptable behaviour in young animals so that I can try to get the owners on the right track before it is too late, and euthanasia has to be considered.

Sometimes when a pet is suffering from an incurable condition there is no other possible decision. One of the hardest parts of being a vet is having to do this and deal with the owners over it. But it is necessary and we all have to face it. It still sometimes comes as a shock and brings a tear to the eye. Cas, a boxer, was still a relatively young dog at eight years old, and not apparently particularly unwell, but as is often the case, Mr and Mrs Ventriss, Cas's owners, had felt that something was not quite right with him and brought him along for a check-up. In his history there was little to go on. He was a bit lethargic, not eating very well and generally down in the dumps. I checked him over and found little wrong with him. I was puzzled. I was on the point of saying, 'We'll do nothing and see if he gets over it himself,' when Mrs Ventriss said that at home he was much worse than he was in the surgery. He had brightened up by being brought out and meeting all the other dogs in the packed waiting room. This is very common, and on the strength of what Mrs Ventriss had said, I decided to run some routine blood tests. Some of these we could do in-house but others would have to be sent away because our haematology machine was being replaced.

The first set of tests came back normal for kidney and liver function so I thought no more of it. Perhaps the owners were being over-anxious. A few days later they were back: Cas had made no progress and, if anything, was more lethargic. I had requested a faxed report on the second set of tests and I popped into my office to see if it had arrived. By coincidence at that moment it was coming through the machine and I waited a few minutes. I scanned through the results and thought at first that there must be a misprint. A white cell count of 210,000? The maximum should be 17,000. I looked at it more closely: all the white cells consisted of cancerous lymphocytes and there at the side was the haematologist's sympathetic comment: 'Sorry, this dog has leukaemia.'

I was stunned. I had not expected this and now I had to break the news. The outlook with a white cell count this high was hopeless. Bone-marrow transplants are not possible in dogs and any attempt at chemotherapy would cause tumour lysis syndrome in which the cancer cells die and cause the kidneys and circulation to clog up, which leads to rapid death. There was nothing I could do for Cas. We would be able to keep him comfortable for a short time and then, in a week or two when the inevitable deterioration set in, put him to sleep.

I went back into the consulting room where the owners were chatting to each other, blissfully unaware of the news I was about to give them. I repeated the words of the haematologist and Mrs Ventriss burst into tears. I was feeling choked up myself, and everyone was upset for the dog and his owners. I had to explain that Cas's case was hopeless, and that even in humans with the possibility of bone-marrow transplants the outlook is always guarded. We wondered whether we should let Cas go now, but it seemed too harsh and his owners needed time to come to terms with the situation. He wasn't in any pain so I put him on antibiotics to help with the infections that would come along, and we arranged for him to have weekly check-ups. In this sort of situation, it is a definite bonus to have Rolf Harris around as he always goes out of his way to comfort grief-stricken owners.

Over the next few weeks Cas went gradually downhill, lost his appetite and became even more lethargic. Early one morning, less than a month later, he was obviously in the last stages. His grieving owners brought him in and he was given an injection to help him out of his suffering.

Cas's case reminded me of the advice given to me by one of my college professors early in my training: 'Listen carefully to the owners – they know their pet best.' At first sight I wouldn't have dreamed that Cas's illness could be so serious, and I was glad that I had decided to act on Mrs Ventriss's own feelings. As a result we were quickly on to the diagnosis which gave us all a little time to accept what would have to happen and be prepared for it.

Many owners are observant and pick up small lumps and bumps amazingly quickly, while others bring in their animals with huge inoperable cancers that must have existed for months, maintaining that they have only just noticed them. The common feature, I suppose, is fear of cancer. Mostly it is unfounded because the majority of lumps are non-malignant and easily cured by surgery. Every now and then, though, that isn't the case and this was the story with Freddie. His owner, Mrs Knight, had noticed a small non-healing ulcer on his scrotum. After it had failed to clear up with simple creams from the chemist, she brought him in to us. Freddie was as fine a specimen of German shepherd as you would wish to see and with a lovely temperament to match. When I first qualified as a vet, German shepherds were generally regarded with suspicion, often neurotic and fear-biters. That has changed and, for the most part, the temperament defects have been successfully bred out of them. Generally they are intelligent, amenable to training and faithful companions – in fact one of my favourite breeds of dog.

Freddie, no exception, rolled over cheerfully on to his back and allowed me to inspect the ulcer. It looked angry: it was very inflamed with a tendency to bleed when touched. I didn't like the look of it at all. I thought it might be cancerous and straight away performed a simple test: I pressed a microscope slide against the ulcer, stained it, and looked at it under the microscope. The whole procedure takes only five minutes and Mrs Knight waited while I did it to see if the test proved positive.

Under the microscope I found thousands of 'mast' cells. There was my diagnosis: it was a mast cell tumour and this was potentially disastrous news because it can be a rapidly fatal form of cancer. These tumours are often malignant, meaning that they can spread elsewhere in the body – usually to the liver and lungs but also anywhere else. I would have to remove the tumour with very wide margins to minimise the risk of spread and fatality. In Freddie's case this meant removing the entire scrotum – a much bigger operation than castration. I arranged to do it the next day.

Everything went to plan and Freddie went home afterwards as I knew he would be well looked after. I sent off the tumour for examination in the laboratory, to confirm my diagnosis and also to let me know what degree of malignancy we could expect, and ultimately therefore, Freddie's outlook. Although the initial test had given us a warning of the diagnosis, a stained section of the actual cancer would be the most accurate way to find out what his chances were. By looking at the cancer cells, and seeing how fast they were dividing, the histopathologist would be able to tell me how malignant it was. I felt pretty confident, nevertheless, that I had caught it in time, and said so to Mrs Knight.

A few days later I received an urgent fax from the laboratory. Examination had confirmed the diagnosis but warned me to start chemotherapy right away since the tumour was of the most malignant type with a poor outlook. I looked at the words 'poor outlook' with frank disbelief. How would I break the news to the owner? She had not long lost her husband, also from cancer. She put a brave face on it, although I could tell she was very upset. We decided to put Freddie on high doses of steroids for a month and see how things went. Steroids are considered among the best treatments for mast cell tumours, and more advanced types of drug were not thought to give any improved chance. Even so, I still hoped that the pathologist had been wrong and that all would be well.

A month later all seemed well. Freddie's wound had healed well, he seemed bright and he was eating everyone out of house and home, and drinking lots of water – common side effects from the steroids. I thought it safe to reduce his dose of steroids and check in another month, but a few weeks later Freddie was

back. He had started to vomit blood and was passing
black motions. Worse still, I found a lump where his
scrotum had been. I couldn't believe it. The cancer had
returned in spite of a huge incision round the original
ulcer. I was pretty sure that the vomiting of blood was
due to ulceration in the intestinal tract, which is
usually associated with the spread of a mast-cell
tumour.

I had to decide whether to fight on or give in, and
that also depended on Mrs Knight. We looked at
Freddie and came to the same conclusion. It would be
wrong to continue. Brave though she was, the tears
began to flow. She held him while I injected the
pentobarbitone into a vein. It was less than two
months since I had first diagnosed his illness. It had
been one of the worst tumours I had ever seen for rapid
spread, even after an early diagnosis and radical
surgery. I was very upset.

A few months later Mrs Knight was back to see me
with a bottle of wine and a new puppy, another
beautiful German shepherd. I gave him his first
vaccination and hoped he would live thirteen or
fourteen years . He had certainly found himself a good
home and it was lovely to see his owner so cheerful and
optimistic. She had come through so much and I
admired her fighting spirit. Having a new pet is really
the only way to get over the heartache of losing one,
but it's not something a vet can suggest. It is a decision
that only the owner can make. Once the new arrival is
installed though, the sadness lifts rapidly. Of course,
they don't replace the departed pet, but after a time
they find their own equally important place in your

life. Mrs Knight's new puppy was also called Freddie, and I looked forward to seeing him over the years sitting patiently in the waiting room showing the other dogs how to behave.

Behaviour is a combination of training with basic temperament, and I'm often struck by the fact that calm dogs usually have calm owners – and sometimes the reverse is true. Oddly enough, pets often come to look like their owners, and I'm not sure why this is, but it is quite common for a fat owner to have a fat pet. This was the downfall of Gazza, Michael's dog. Most people know who the ultimate Gazza is, if they're British anyway. He is, of course, Paul Gascoigne, a great England footballer and, like many footballers with a nickname, many dogs are named after him. Gascoigne once suffered an appalling injury in a cup final after a hard tackle: he ruptured his anterior cruciate ligament – one of the most important ligaments in the knee. The cruciate ligaments, anterior and posterior, cross over inside the knee joint. They are called cruciate from the Latin meaning cross. It is usually the anterior one that is damaged and a rupture is a severe injury. Apart from footballers, skiers and dogs are also at risk. In dogs it is normally seen in the middle-aged, overweight and lethargic, like Gazza, who stood in front of me on the consulting table.

A nine-year-old Labrador retriever, he had once been as fit as his namesake, but over the last few years he had become a bit of a couch potato and preferred eating to exercise. This had suited his owner, Michael, a pensioner with arthritis. On 1 January that year Michael had decided to lose weight, fight the arthritis and get fitter. He planned to go swimming three times weekly, and take Gazza out twice a day for walks in the park.

All went well until one Sunday afternoon a few weeks later in the local park. It was cold and icy and the squirrels were hungry, coming quite close and begging for food. Gazza took off after one of them and sprinted about a hundred yards, only to see the squirrel race up a tree. He made one last jump, snapping at its tail, and twisted as he landed. He gave a loud yelp and immediately started to limp slowly to Michael, who had shouted in vain for him to come back. Few dogs will obey their masters once they are in full cry after something as tempting as a squirrel, unless they have been to advanced training classes. It was obvious that Gazza had done himself a mischief, as he was not putting any weight on the leg. Michael made his way home and had a look at the leg. He could see no obvious injury, no cuts or bruises, so thought that perhaps Gazza had pulled a muscle. He decided to wait and see, and gave the dog his evening meal, which being a Labrador, he ate. Virtually *nothing* puts them off food!

The next day Gazza seemed a bit better so Michael left it a little longer, but a few days later when the dog was still limping he brought him to the hospital. We lifted Gazza onto the table, where he immediately put on a sorry-looking face, while trying to pretend I wasn't there as I prodded him around. He had the typical stance of the cruciate rupture, nearly 100 per cent lame, his toes just touching the ground. His knee joint, or stifle, was too painful to manipulate and I booked him in for an anaesthetic so that I could have a good look and feel. Then we weighed him: 42 kilos – far too much! It was double misery for poor old Gazza: strict rations and trips to the vet.

When we X-rayed him and felt him under anaesthetic my diagnosis was confirmed and I knew we would have to operate or Gazza might end up with the same complaint as his owner – arthritis.

The operation was similar to the one the dog's famous namesake underwent, and involved using a piece of tissue from the outside of the muscle as a new ligament, which was threaded through the interior of the joint. We do this almost weekly at the hospital and it takes just under an hour. Stan performed the surgery, about five weeks later, by which time Gazza had reduced to a trimmer 33 kilos. After an initial ten days' rest, he was put on a programme of gradually increasing exercise on the lead. This benefited him and his owner, and I was delighted to see him looking fit and well with only a slight limp some six weeks after the operation. Three months later he had completely recovered. Michael had lost three stone, which meant that he also suffered far less pain, so what had appeared a disaster at the time turned out to have been a blessing for both of them. It was a funny thing but Gazza seemed to lose all interest in squirrels after that episode. Even if they were within easy distance he wouldn't give them a second glance.

If only all pets and their problems were as straightforward as Gazza and his cruciate injury. Occasionally people bring parrots to the hospital, which I don't enjoy much because, like most vets, I don't know a lot about them. They usually need to see a specialist: it's difficult enough for the vet in small-animal practice to keep up to date with what's going on in that field, let alone having to learn about bird diseases in general and parrot ones in particular. However, we usually have a look before we refer a case elsewhere. A knowledge of bird disease takes years of study and I have devoted the last twenty years to getting to grips with skin complaints – but not in parrots!

Freddy – yes, another one! – was suffering from feather loss so I took the basic history as we do with any animal. It was not easy in Freddy's case because he was owned by an Italian lady, whose English was a little difficult to understand. 'What do you feed him?' I asked.

'Well, I feed him spaghetti, because I am Italian,' said the lady, with obvious pride, 'and some time he no like this so I give him curry.''

'Curry?' I echoed, hardly believing my ears. I had thought I had heard most things in my time since qualification – but a curry-eating parrot?

'Yes, he love curry.'

Just then Freddy, as though to prove the point, let out a long, cackling laugh. Within minutes everyone within hearing distance, including people in the waiting room, was laughing too. The more we laughed, the more cackling we got from Freddy, and it took five minutes before we could get on with the consultation. Rolf with a twinkle in his eye asked if I was going to get him out to examine him.

I knew I should advise Freddy's owner that a parrot

needed a parrot diet, not a human one, but before I could do this I had to examine the bird. Easier said than done. We had been warned that Freddy did not like being handled. I started by enticing him out of his cage to sit on his owner's shoulder. Then I approached him gingerly and tried to stroke him. Freddy interpreted this as an attack on his owner and responded by shrieking and making furious, aggressive pecking attacks.

An alternative plan was called for. This consisted of throwing a towel over the bird's head and trying to hold him with his wings close to his chest. Failure. Freddy was now emitting ear-piercing shrieks, which were accompanied by his owner shouting at him to behave.

We were rapidly losing control and as I made a further attempt to handle Freddy he confirmed my suspicion by taking a large chunk out of my thumb. The pain was as excruciating as it had been with the ferret bite, but I hung on, pinioned his wings to his side and got him under reasonable restraint. Now I had to examine his wings to try to assess the degree of feather loss, but she wriggled free and nipped another lump out of my hand. Handling parrots is definitely a job for experts! When I did manage to get a decent look at him, it didn't help me much because I couldn't find anything abnormal.

Apparently parrot experts take lots of samples, including blood, and there is a standard way to investigate feather loss. I found that out later in the day when I made a few phone calls to vets who are acknowledged experts in this field. The veterinary profession is lucky in that it is small and, generally speaking, you can get advice on almost any topic just by picking up the phone. Meanwhile, Freddy's owner and I decided that Freddy would be fed proper parrot food and we would see how things went. I handed over a diet sheet and sent them off with a sigh of relief. They left me feeling inadequate, as far as parrots were concerned, and nursing several painful bites in my hand.

A few weeks later, Freddy returned. His owner said he was improving and relishing his new diet. This time he was examined by our locum Richard – I kept a low profile – who gave the owner the address of a vet in Essex who knows all about parrots in the event that Freddy's improvement was not maintained.

Parrots are used to the freedom of the jungle and if they are to be kept in captivity then they are probably best off in large, specialised aviaries with masses of room in which to fly. Also, their owners should develop a detailed knowledge of how they should be looked after, so think several times before you decide to take one on. It is easy to buy a parrot but if the bird lacks the correct environment it will probably end up with a dull, unhealthy lifestyle. A parrot may lose its feathers through boredom: if it has nothing to do in a too-small cage, it will sit around all day pulling out its feathers. Some sad parrots pluck themselves completely bald.

The patient after Freddy was more in my line and baldness wasn't her problem. It seemed more sinister. Marigold Serendipity Diamond Tourmaline first came as a patient when she was fifteen years old. Her owner,

Joyce, was tearful. She and Marigold had been together for so many years that she was one of the family and it seemed now that her cat had come to the end of her life. It wasn't so much that she was ill – far from it, I thought, as she took a swipe at me while I was examining her. It was the presence of a large growth on her side that was worrying us. When I had last looked at it we had decided to leave it as she was getting on, but now the tumour had grown to the point where either something had to be done about it or Marigold would have to be put down. The tumour occupied her whole side. Could I remove it? Would she survive the anaesthetic? What type of tumour was it? Would it spread if I attempted removal? These were the questions going through my mind as I examined the cat.

Marigold was getting increasingly fed up as I worked on her and I could hardly hear her heart through the stethoscope for the growls and hisses. And what did Joyce want to do about it? Her face showed that she was expecting the worst. I had a think. The tumour was unlikely to be malignant as there was no sign of spread to any other area or organs and it had been there for some time. Marigold was well otherwise, and fit for a general anaesthetic. We could find out the long-term prognosis only by operating and sending the growth for analysis. The remaining question was how long she could live after the operation. No guarantees here, but I felt at least three months, maybe more – no promises. Joyce didn't hesitate for an instant. Her face lit up and we scheduled the operation for a week hence.

Getting Marigold anaesthetised was the first hurdle:

she was extremely uncooperative. But, eventually, she was all prepped up, looking helpless and vulnerable – a total contrast to the teeth and claws of five minutes earlier. The tumour was difficult to remove as there was hardly enough skin to close the wound afterwards, but an hour later Marigold was looking like a piggy bank with a long suture wound down her side. I was pretty sure that I had got out all the tumour and I sent it off to the histopathologist for examination. I knew the results of the test on it would tell me what type of tumour it was and how it was likely to behave. It would also confirm whether I had been successful in removing it all, as the pathologist would look at the edges of the tumour to see if normal cancer-free tissue was present.

I sent Marigold home after the surgery and then we had to wait. I knew that Joyce would be worrying herself sick, so I phoned the histopathologist a couple of days later. As luck would have it, she had just finished looking at the sections.

The next day I saw Marigold and passed on the news to Joyce. It was both good and bad. The good news was that the tumour had been removed well and was not malignant. The bad news was that this particular type of tumour, a fibrosarcoma, often recurs, even if it appears to have been completely removed, and it is much harder to remove a second time. That is true for most cancers, and it is often said that the first operation has the best chance of success. Another saying, equally true, of skin cancers, which I learned from an American vet who specialises in tumour surgery is: 'Find 'em small and treat 'em big.'

Marigold had recovered well and a week later I took out her stitches. 'She'll see Christmas,' I told Joyce, 'but after that who knows?' I have learned over the years not to make predictions on animals' life-spans as you can never rely on them. Naturally people are upset if you get it wrong and a pet dies suddenly but on the other hand they delight in telling their friends that the vet said that the pet would be dead in three months and five years later here she is, still alive. Best to take as a bonus each month as it comes, particularly with old animals.

Nevertheless by Christmas it was clear that Marigold was going to last some time, so I told Joyce to come back if she was worried and expected to see her a few months later. Imagine my surprise to see her in the waiting room nearly three *years* later with an only slightly older-looking Marigold. There had been no sign of recurrence of the tumour until now. But it had come back in exactly the same place, where I felt an ominous hard swelling. Marigold was now coming up to eighteen so we had to make the difficult decision as to whether or not to operate again. I decided to go ahead and a few days later the cat was in ward three coming round after I had removed the growth. I sent off a sample to the histopathologist but I was fairly certain that it was a fibrosarcoma and two days later this was confirmed. 'This will be the last time,' I told Joyce, 'so we'll have to keep our fingers crossed.'

Three months later, though, there was another lump on Marigold's side. It was the first time that she had been filmed so I updated Rolf on her story. Fibrosarcomas don't respond to chemotherapy so I could do nothing more, and I didn't think it would be right to put the cat through another operation. Neither did her owner. I told Joyce to keep her as long as possible and when the time came we would put her to sleep.

Three months later Marigold was back and I was expecting the worst – but an incredible thing had happened. The tumour had all but disappeared! What a survivor this cat was! Some things are hard to explain but I suppose that somehow her immune system had got on top of it and it had regressed. Failure or weakness of the immune system may be at the root of most tumours, especially when they occur in old animals. I have seen similar regressions over the years when animals have recovered from usually fatal conditions completely against the odds.

However, at Marigold's age, I felt the tumour might come back again, especially if she developed any other illness. A few months later she showed signs of kidney disease: she lost weight, went off her food and began to drink a lot. Again I could feel the swelling on her side. This time I held out little hope: Marigold was in a gentle but irreversible decline. I gave her the usual treatment for kidney disease but felt that we shouldn't interfere too much. Joyce and I agreed that we would not hang on too long and that I would tell her when I thought Marigold had had enough.

I had forgotten Marigold's fighting spirit and over the next two months she responded to treatment and reached her nineteenth birthday, the tumour growing only very slowly. Four years before I would have been astonished if I had been told that she would survive for so long. That cat simply had a tremendous will to live. The end came suddenly. I had warned Joyce that when Marigold started to go downhill it would probably happen quickly, and a few weeks after her nineteenth birthday she would not eat, became very thirsty and lethargic. Her kidneys had failed. I did not feel that any further investigation was warranted. A small injection and she fell asleep, without knowing what had happened. Joyce was so brave – I expect the tears came later. I couldn't help feeling that Marigold had been a very lucky cat, had had a lovely life with a doting owner, and in her nineteenth year a peaceful ending – something I would wish for all animals.

CHAPTER EIGHT

Some Common Problems

I remember well my first clinic as a newly qualified vet. My head was full of complex diseases, whose symptoms I had memorised by heart, and every case seemed baffling. When I settled down, though, I began to realise that common problems are so-called for the simple reason that you see them over and over again. Many conditions occur so frequently that you have to be careful not to be blasé about them and perhaps miss something else.

Many common diseases should be rare: the ones that

are preventable by vaccination. In the UK a significant number of dogs and cats are unvaccinated and over half of those that have been treated don't receive regular boosters. Don't forget to take your pet along to the vet once a year for its jabs – it could make the difference between life and death.

One such disease is kennel cough and one afternoon I saw such a spate of cases that I wondered if we were in the midst of an epidemic. The name of the condition is misleading as it implies that it is only caught in kennels. This is not so as most kennels are well managed: the dogs are vaccinated before entry and sufficiently well isolated from each other. The disease is highly contagious and will be transmitted from dog to dog wherever they meet up.

Jason was my first case of the afternoon, a huge floppy young golden retriever. He had been coughing for several days and kept up his owners – a family of two parents and two young children – awake for much of the previous night. The whole family trooped in looking anxious. Little Lisa, aged three, looked as though she was going to cry. As they walked in, Jason bounded over, jumped up, and barked playfully, which set him off in a deep throaty cough. It lasted a minute and at the end of the spasm he spat out a little phlegm. The older daughter, Jennifer, was convinced that Jason had swallowed a bone as he had been caught raiding the dustbin. He was her dog, and she had chosen him herself on her sixth birthday. She spent most of her time with him and answered my questions.

'Is he still eating and swallowing without any problems?' I asked.

'Oh, yes, he still loves his food!'

'And he's still very playful – in fact he doesn't seem very ill at all,' her mother added. 'It's just this dreadful cough – he sounds like a smoker first thing in the morning!' This was said with a meaningful glance at her husband who, by all accounts had been trying to give up for several months after a nasty chest infection.

I checked Jason over. In between sloppy kisses and wrestling matches I established that he wasn't really ill. I checked down his throat but couldn't see any sign of a bone or other foreign body. In all probability there wasn't one, although you can get caught out. A useful test to check for kennel cough is to squeeze the dog's larynx gently, which often sets up the typical cough. Jason obliged and I told the owners that I thought it most likely that he had kennel cough. As Jason hadn't been vaccinated, I explained how we would have to treat him. 'I'll put him on some antibiotics and if you're lucky he'll be much better in about ten days,' I said. 'Otherwise the cough may drag on for several weeks – and I may need to give him some tranquillisers to ensure that he can get some sleep.'

One of the bugs that causes kennel cough is called *Bordetella bronchiseptica* and can be hard to shift, hence the warning to Jason's owners. A different type of *Bordetella* – *pertussis* – is the cause of whooping cough in children. Fortunately the two diseases are quite distinct and cannot be transmitted from dog to human and vice versa.

Jason would need plenty of nursing – I knew he would get that, and several other things would help. A choke chain can precipitate coughing – and a better form of restraint is a Halti which can be bought at most pet shops. It is a type of muzzle that fits round the snout and closes when pulled, gently averting the head. It is a good training device for dogs that pull and is useful as a general restraint. Jason should not be subjected to sudden changes between warm and cold air, and must be kept out of smoky atmospheres. As I mentioned this, the whole family turned on Dad and I felt that his smoking days were probably over, at least in the house. 'And don't forget he's infectious to other dogs,' I finished. Fortunately Jason had sat in the car rather than in the waiting room while waiting his turn to be seen because he tended to get overexcited in the company of other dogs. Once he was better he would need proper training, and a full course of vaccinations.

Two hours later, near the end of the outpatient session, I was examining what looked like my fourth case of kennel cough that day. This was Rex, a Rottweiler who, apart from his appearance – which was enough to strike terror into anyone's heart – was a most genial dog. Placid and resigned to being prodded by the vet, he had already had to endure an hour or so surrounded by yapping dogs and their impatient owners. He had been coughing for several weeks and seemed a bit slower than usual, but was eating quite well and in all other respects was perfectly normal.

Like the others he coughed when I pressed his larynx. He also took exception to this indignity and began a series of warning growls. This was unfortunate, because I had to spend the next part of his examination listening to his chest. I was a bit too close to his teeth for comfort anyway, but the growling made it difficult to hear the heart and lungs – through a stethoscope, it sounds like a motorbike revving up. In between growls, the heart sounded fine if a little fast. Five minutes later Rex was plodding out with his owner, a young man who obviously thought the world of his dog, and a ten-day course of antibiotics, which the owner explained he would only be able to get down Rex with Toblerone, his favourite chocolate!

Ten days later I saw the results of my treatment. Two of the kennel cough cases, including Jason, were almost clear, one was making good progress, but still coughing at night – he needed an extra week of antibiotics. But Rex was worse. The cough had deepened, was worse on exercise and had increased at night. Now his owner wasn't sleeping well either, as the dog spent the nights in his bedroom.

Rex was more lethargic than last time and couldn't have cared less about me, whatever I did, so there was no growling. This time I had a good listen to his chest and his lungs sounded clear. But his heart was clearly abnormal. It was beating fast, which couldn't be down to nerves as he was even more placid than usual. It was chaotic, and varied from loud to soft beats, a waxing and waning sound. I checked his pulse: it bore no relation to the heart rate, and was slow and irregular. This suggested that the heart, although beating very fast and erratically, was inefficient and only the relatively few strong beats – strong enough to give a good pulse – were getting through to the circulation. I was now sure that we weren't dealing with kennel cough and admitted Rex straight away. He was put on the afternoon list for an X-ray and an

ECG. X-rays are useful in assessing dogs and cats for heart disease as you can see the size of the heart quite clearly; when it is diseased it often enlarges. The ECG, or electrocardiograph, measures the electrical activity of the heart, showing up in particular abnormalities in the rhythm. I suspected that Rex might have a heart disease called atrial fibrillation, often caused by a serious defect of the heart muscles. I hoped that the ECG and X-ray would confirm this. With hindsight, I should have realised that kennel cough wasn't very likely because Rex was older than the dogs I had seen with it when I first met him.

That afternoon Gabriel, who had been at the Harmsworth a year and was keen on cardiology, did the tests. The results were dramatic: the X-rays showed that Rex's heart was very enlarged. It is a common sign of a failing heart, which either fills up with too much blood, or sometimes the heart muscles get bigger as it tries to compensate for its failure in efficiency. Rex's heart occupied most of his chest, and was pushing the main airway up near his spine. We had to sedate him to get a good tracing on the ECG before we lifted him carefully on to the operating table. This was no mean achievement as he weighed more than 50 kilos and every now and then tried to sit up to see what was going on.

Later, when Gabriel and I pored over it the ECG tracing confirmed what I had suspected: an abnormal rhythm of the heart, atrial fibrillation, which means that the pacemaker does not function and the chambers of the heart, the atria, contract too fast while the ventricles, which power the blood to the lungs and all over the body, do not follow a steady rhythm.

Next day Gabriel explained this to Rex's owner. The underlying cause of the condition was probably a disease of the heart muscles, cardiomyopathy. The condition is poorly understood, and also occurs in humans – it is one reason why some patients have heart transplants. Heart transplants are not possible in clinical practice in veterinary medicine, so Rex would have to be managed with medical treatment. He was given digoxin to slow the heart rate and make the heartbeat stronger and more efficient, and also lasix, which helps disperse the excess fluid that accumulates when the heart is not functioning properly. While the drugs were taking effect he would need rest.

His anxious owner had to be told that, sadly, the long-term outlook was not good and that it would be unlikely that Rex would survive for another year. The diagnosis of heart disease is always upsetting for a pet owner. Many worry that their animal will have a heart attack and drop dead. Fortunately, in dogs and cats, heart attacks as we know them in humans are almost unheard of and they do not usually die suddenly. Much more common is a story of gradual deterioration, and sometimes the pet lives long enough to die of something else.

This, I thought, would probably be the case with Lucy, an eight-year-old Cavalier King Charles spaniel. She was the very patient I saw after Rex.

Lucy had been brought to the hospital because she had started panting out on walks and coughed after running in the park. Otherwise she was bright. It didn't take long to establish what her problem was. She had a heart murmur: this is caused by a leaky heart valve, most commonly the valve between the atria and the ventricles on the left side of the heart. When you are listening to a normal heart, you will hear the valves shut with a sharp, rhythmic click. If there is a leak instead of a sharp click you will hear a swooshing sound as the blood leaks back into the ventricle. The swooshing is called a murmur and I could hear this clearly in Lucy's chest.

I turned to tell Lucy's owner the diagnosis. Mrs Pritchard's husband had died the week before from a heart attack. I explained gently that King Charles spaniels commonly have heart murmurs, and I had seen thousands in my time, but Lucy would have to have treatment for the rest of her life.

'How long has she got?' Mrs Pritchard asked.

I replied, 'Hopefully many years yet. There's no reason why at her age – eight – she shouldn't go on to eleven or more.' I couldn't be certain of that but there was no point in making Mrs Pritchard miserable with worry, and in any case I didn't expect Lucy to die suddenly in the near future. The disease was in its early stages and normally if the dog is going to deteriorate there are plenty of warning signs. I prescribed a fairly mild heart and circulation stimulant to start with and said, 'Try not to worry. I know it's difficult but there are some very good drugs on the market and I can see no reason why we can't make Lucy's life just about normal. The only down side is that you'll have to see my ugly face every couple of months!' Mrs Pritchard smiled, but it took some months for her to begin to relax. Lucy's condition is a well-recognised problem in dogs and can be satisfactorily managed now. She is still living with it quite happily.

Another disease that never goes away is parvo virus. We have an entire isolation ward with the capacity to hold ten dogs with this disease and, at worst, it is full. Parvo virus didn't exist when I first qualified: it appeared suddenly during the 1980s, first in America then explosively in the UK and later world-wide. The consequences were dreadful. I was in private practice at the time and we were overwhelmed with cases.

Initially no vaccine was available but it was discovered fairly quickly that the virus was similar to one that causes feline enteritis and that the vaccine against that disease conferred some resistance. We worked long hours trying to protect all our clients' animals. Of all the diseases I have come across in animals as a vet it is one of the worst. The vaccine now available is virtually 100 per cent solid, so make sure that your pet has its jab. If everyone had their dogs vaccinated, the disease could probably be eradicated. We see hundreds of cases at the Harmsworth, with one common characteristic: the dogs that become ill have not been vaccinated.

Spike, a fifteen-week-old Staffordshire bull terrier, was typical. His owner brought him in when he had been vomiting for two days. He was miserable and listless, dehydrated, and after I had taken his temperature the thermometer showed traces of blood. Not much doubt about the diagnosis: the symptoms of parvo virus are vomiting and bloody diarrhoea. Without treatment many dogs die, and even with treatment about 20 per cent do not survive.

I asked Mrs Smith if Spike had been vaccinated. She broke down, and told me that he hadn't yet and he had been out in the streets. She hadn't realised that parvo virus is so resistant and is everywhere in the environment, and had thought that a few little walks outside the house could not do her dog any harm. We now had a battle on our hands and I had to tell Mrs Smith that Spike would need a week of intensive treatment and it would be touch and go, especially in the first few days.

Over the last ten years treatment for this disease has become standardised. First, and most important, we put up a drip to counteract any dehydration. Then we give injections to suppress the vomiting and antibiotics for any secondary infection. Treatment of parvo virus is a succession of triumphs and setbacks, and sometimes failure. The next day Spike was much worse, passing pure blood and looking depressed. There is nothing that can be done in these circumstances except to step up the fluids and hope that the puppy has enough strength to keep going. Spike had plenty of strength so I didn't despair. As we entered the third day Spike was very weak and still vomiting, but at least he had stopped passing blood. We had to get the vomiting under control, though, and start Spike on oral fluids. After five days he had reached this stage and I was confident. However, after a week we had to put him back on a drip as he started to vomit again. This is so typical of the disease: you think you have it cracked and then you go back to square one. But each day that passes is a good sign and the longer we can keep the dog alive the more likely it is that the it will pull through.

At last, after nine days, Spike turned the corner and started to demand food in no uncertain terms. It is so satisfying to see a severely ill puppy suddenly show signs of recovery. The nurses started him with a light diet of fish, chicken and rice, and a day or so later he was fit to go home. One lucky dog.

Parvo virus is not the only disease with diarrhoea and vomiting – or D and V, as we call it. Mostly D and V is caused by a tummy upset, but we have to make sure that the patient is not suffering from parvo, or even a foreign body in the intestine, which will require surgery.

Given half a chance, dogs will make pigs of themselves, just like some humans, and as a vet if you want intensive experience of D and V in dogs and cats you should volunteer for duty at Christmas, or more especially Boxing Day, which is when the results of excess become apparent. I have seen dogs who have eaten the entire turkey, while the family was at church, others who have eaten several boxes of chocolates all at once and a kitten that lapped up a cup of a well-known alcoholic cream liqueur – afterwards it slept for thirty-six hours under observation in the hospital but went on to make a full recovery!

For the most part you can tell the straightforward D and V cases because the animal is not usually unwell and the owner often reports some sudden change in its diet. It happens frequently when a kitten or puppy is brought home for the first time and put on a strange diet. The standard approach with all these patients is to starve them for twenty-four hours, giving just fluids little and often, then to introduce a light diet, such as chicken or fish and rice for three or four days. This usually does the trick, but if it doesn't, we have to investigate further.

Bruno's owner had already tried our usual treatment before bringing him to the hospital. A two-year-old boxer, he had demonstrated several times that he was prone to tummy upsets: unless he was watched very closely he ate literally anything: the contents of dustbins – he was an expert in knocking them over and getting the lid off – bits of bread in the park, the cat's food (a special delicacy), whatever he could find. After he had been scavenging, his stomach would swell before his owner's eyes, a prelude to the inevitable attack of D and V that followed. In fact his owner Steve, a student, had learned to recognise the early signs and put paper everywhere to simplify the clearing up.

After the third or fourth episode we ran some tests on Bruno to see if there was any reason for his greed, but everything showed up normal and we concluded that food was his passion. And it wasn't just food: Steve had come home recently and found that Bruno had drunk a lot of his home-made beer, having managed to get his head into the barrel. This hadn't caused a tummy upset but had made him very quiet for the rest of the evening, and he hadn't wanted to go far on his walk.

Bruno was my last case in a busy afternoon surgery and when I heard that it was D and V again I thought he'd soon be over it. However, as soon as I took a look at him I felt that something wasn't quite right. Bruno wasn't his usual exuberant self – even with a tummy upset he would bound into the surgery and often jump up on the table, which few other dogs do. That day it was as much as he could do to walk in and he flop down with a sigh.

'How long has he been like this, Steve?' I asked.

'Only the last day or so. He raided my neighbour's dustbin three days ago and he's still vomiting. And he won't touch his food.'

Bruno not interested in food? Something *must* be wrong. 'What about diarrhoea?' I asked.

Steve thought for a minute. 'There hasn't been any in the last twenty-four hours. Do you think something's got stuck?' This was exactly what I was thinking. We lifted Bruno on to the table. He was far too depressed and looked too ill for this to be his usual tummy upset. His temperature was normal but his rectum was empty suggesting that nothing was being passed. Of real significance, though, was his pulse, which was thin and weak, nothing like the full, bounding, strong pulse of a healthy boxer. I pressed his lips to check his capillary refill and monitor the circulation. It was sluggish. Finally I felt his tummy. He was sore, no doubt about that, and too tense for me to gain any useful information. All the signs pointed to a foreign body and I told Steve we would have to have Bruno in for X-rays and an examination under anaesthetic.

The vomiting had dehydrated him and the nurse put up a fluid drip, which he would have needed anyway before an operation, which was now looking increasingly likely. Then I sedated him lightly so that he would lie still on the X-ray plate and took a picture. The result wasn't dramatically obvious but there was a lot of gas in Bruno's intestines and the suggestion of a lump. Enough to justify opening him up.

It was now late afternoon and tomorrow's list was horrendous – best to get on with the operation right away. Just a few ccs of the intravenous anaesthetic thiopentone to knock him out, and then we put a tube into his larynx, through which the gas would be passed. Liz, the nurse prepared Bruno for his operation, which involved clipping all the hair from his abdomen – not a very big job as boxers are all chest. Then she sterilised the skin with iodine solution and surgical spirit.

The surgical incision was in the mid-line and immediately I was through into the abdomen via the peritoneum. Within minutes I had localised a hard lump in Bruno's intestines and managed to get it in view. About five inches of intestine was red and angry-looking with a large object inside it. What could it be? Liz and I began to take bets. Some kind of rubber toy was my guess. Liz thought it might be plastic. We were both wrong. A few minutes later the object was lying on a piece of gauze. It was a corn-on-the-cob.

The operation didn't last more than three-quarters of an hour, but poor old Bruno had to spend a couple of days with us and he didn't enjoy the first. He had fluids in the vein, with nil by mouth. On the second day he was allowed to drink a special rehydrating fluid, little and often, and then, on the third day, he had a little chicken. On day two he was his usual boisterous and hungry self, barking incessantly and begging whenever a nurse passed by. By the third we were pleading with Steve to come and get him so we could have a bit of peace and quiet in ward two.

Predictably Bruno made a full recovery and Steve resolved to keep him on a tighter rein to try to prevent further episodes. Bruno was a delightful dog but he looked like one of those who doesn't slow down until they are eight or nine. Most pets are hard work, especially in their first year, but I reckon that persistent good training usually pays off by the time they are two, which is what I found with my own dog, Barney.

Acquiring a puppy or kitten can be a joy for the whole family, especially the children, but there is a steep learning curve for everyone. The adults must make sure that the little creature has the proper food and care, while the children must learn that the new addition is not a toy: it has feelings and needs too. The pet, perhaps, is on the steepest learning curve of all as it works out how to live with and adapt to family life. If things go wrong, as they often do if the pet has been acquired from an unsatisfactory source, it can be devastatingly worrying – as in Lacey's case. In this instance not only was the puppy not well but he caused problems in his owner too.

Lacey was a lovely little puppy who had been bought from a pet shop. Although he was only about six weeks old he had a serious skin disease. Since his owner had acquired him, he had done nothing but scratch, and his owner had developed a severe rash, which was all over his chest and abdomen and was intolerable at night in bed. He told me that from the beginning the puppy had crept into his bed – no doubt missing his mum.

Actually, lots of pets in England sleep on their owner's bed and sometimes in it, which is fine, except when they develop diseases that can transmit to humans.

I suspected that Lacey, like Snowy earlier, had scabies and that his owner had caught it. It is quite a common disease and the puppy scratched throughout the consultation – most itchy dogs take a break from scratching while they are on the examining table, due to fear, or being overwhelmed, or distracted with curiosity, but Lacey didn't. When I rubbed his ear with my finger and thumb he scratched furiously with his back leg on that side – a pretty sure sign of scabies – and he had lost most of his hair, especially on his legs, face and ears. His owner had a truly spectacular rash all over his chest, which he was only too happy to demonstrate to the cameras.

To prove the diagnosis I found the *Sarcoptes scabiei* mite in skin scrapings. Rolf had a look through the microscope and immediately renamed it Sir Coptes Mite, and drew a cartoon of the dog and his little friend. Skin scraping means just that – you take a scalpel blade, dip it in liquid paraffin and scrape away at the surface of the skin, hoping to catch a mite. The liquid paraffin allows the skin cells and whatever else you pick up to stick to the blade, which makes it easy to transfer it to the microscope slide. The scabies mite is a tiny spherical object, a little smaller than a pin head with four pairs of legs. It looks a bit like a spider, to which family it is related.

Now that we were sure what we were dealing with, the easy part was the treatment. Lacey was given the same shampoos we had given Snowy to kill the mite, and other gentle shampoos to clean his skin. I also advised his owner to spray with an insecticide round the house – particularly his bed: the mite can survive in the environment for a few days and could reinfest both the owner and the puppy.

I was pretty sure that the owner would get better as his puppy improved, but I advised him to see his doctor anyway. Immediately after the programme went out he turned up at the surgery, where the receptionist said, as he walked through the door, 'We know why you're here!'

Three weeks later when I checked Lacey again things were much improved. The little puppy had stopped scratching and his hair was growing through quickly. The owner was free of his rash too – which he proudly demonstrated. I had been expecting him to clear up more quickly than the pup because the dog mite does not like human skin. If the owner keeps away from the pup, the cure is instant , although I still advise owners to see their GP just to be on the safe side. Lesions are always in contact sites such as the abdomen and the mites can crawl through clothing. Another common site is the upper arms if the puppy is carried about.

It was lovely to see Lacey racing around full of the joys of spring and to have helped cure his owner too. Feeling itchy all the time must be miserable – in fact, I have prosecuted several people for neglecting dogs with this condition. I was never able to find out the source of Lacey's infection but many people suspect that foxes pass it on, as scabies is prevalent in the fox population, which has been known for centuries. The medical term 'alopecia', meaning baldness, comes from the Greek *allopekia,* fox. To this day I frequently see injured foxes suffering from the disease. There are foxes all over London so there are plenty of potential hosts for this itchy little mite.

Scabies is not the only skin disease that you might acquire from a pet, although good hygiene and an early trip to the vet as soon as any symptoms appear should minimise the risks. Sometimes, especially with ringworm, there may be so few signs on the pet that the first indication of any trouble is when the owner develops the disease. Ringworm is uncommon in dogs and I only reckon to see half a dozen cases a year, if that. In kittens, though, it is much more common and frequently leads to infection in the owner. In fact, cats are a major source of ringworm in humans, which makes it all the more important to sort out the problem as quickly as possible. Two students brought their kitten in to see me because their GP had diagnosed ringworm in them and suspected that the newly introduced kitten was the source of the infection. They had brought the animal from a pet shop a few weeks earlier, and had suddenly developed big red circular lesions on their arms, which were quite itchy. They told me that they had the same things on their stomachs and thighs, and that the kitten had snuggled up to them in bed.

At first glance the kitten looked normal, although on closer inspection there was some thinning of the fur around the face and ears where the fungus had caused hairs to fall out. Further testing is necessary in such cases so that everybody – vet, doctor and owners – knows where they stand. An accurate diagnosis was what I wanted.

In cats the most useful screening test for ringworm is to shine a special ultraviolet lamp, called the Wood's Lamp, on them. Often, but not always, the affected hairs show up as a bright fluorescent apple green. When I tested the kitten in this way, my diagnosis was virtually confirmed. Nevertheless I also took some samples to grow in the laboratory. In the meantime we had to start treatment, and this was going to be a long, uphill struggle. Treatment for ringworm in cats requires at least six weeks of the fungal antibiotic griseofulvin plus hard work cleaning up the environment where there would be lots of fungal spores, which can remain infectious for up to a year and have to be killed by disinfectants. All the furniture and carpets would need treatment.

I explained everything to the owners who, it turned out, were living with lots of other students in a large house. The kitten had had the run of it and had undoubtedly contaminated most of it. We elected to try steam cleaning with bleach on all the hard surfaces and no cuddling of the kitten for at least six weeks until I could give the all clear.

After three weeks the kitten seemed to be making progress but a couple more students had gone down with the infection. One wasn't even living in the house. Apparently they had had a party and a girl had turned up in a short T-shirt with her midriff bare. During the evening she drank rather a lot and lay face down on the carpet for an hour or so while the effects wore off. A couple of weeks later she developed a classic lesion on her stomach.

Over the next month or so, regular cleaning and continuous treatment for the kitten gradually got us to the stage where I was reasonably confident that we had the infection under control. But it was a full three months before I was certain. I felt that we had been fortunate because ringworm can be tricky to cure and re-infection of both the animal and the owner is common. I shone the Wood's Lamp on the kitten again and took some hair samples for culture. All these tests were negative and I was able to give the official all clear after four months. In the end all ten students had been affected and all had required treatment. Fortunately none had had any problems getting rid of the infection but it had been a worrying time for all concerned.

The commonest cause of skin disease, or for that matter any disease in dogs and cats, is the cat flea, which goes under the exotic name of *Ctenocephalides felis felis*. Fleas have reached epidemic proportions in recent years due to the increasing numbers of pets – particularly cats –which are kept and also our generally increasing standard of living. Fleas love warmth and carpets and these days efficient central heating is the norm, making the average home the ideal environment for flea breeding. The diseases that this pest causes are mainly seen in the skin and there is a variety of clinical signs, especially in the cat.

Since the early sixties fleas have been extensively researched. First, more than two thousand different species have been identified. Then important work proved that, in the main, disease is caused by an allergic reaction to the saliva of the flea when it feeds. Later the insect's life cycle was studied and it was found that fleas have developed ingenious methods to ensure their survival, which vary from species to species. In the last few years efforts have concentrated on how best to eliminate them. Small wonder that this is, therefore, one of the biggest headaches facing vets, especially in the peak months of August, September and October.

About the middle of August each year, almost from one day to the next, the number of people coming through the doors doubles and we are suddenly working flat out to cope with an army of itching dogs and cats. The various syndromes caused by the flea are instantly recognised by experienced vets, although the clinical picture in cats is more difficult to diagnose than it is in dogs, which normally have irritation around the rump with little variability in signs. However, owners almost invariably fail to make the connection and understandably find it difficult to believe the diagnosis. Because the reaction to the flea is mainly allergic in nature, the cat or dog scratches or licks, so the fleas don't stay on the pet. In any case, the main part of the flea's life cycle is spent in the carpets. The average owner will not believe that fleas are the cause of the problem unless they see one, or preferably lots of them.

The two elderly ladies standing before me were classic examples of this. It was at the end of a long afternoon, warm, humid and busy with flea-related cases. Fifi was a middle-aged female cat who was going bald on her back, the backs of her thighs and her belly – classic sites for flea allergy. Fifi had been licking herself due to the irritation, which had caused her hair to be pulled out and hence the baldness. In more severe forms, the constant licking causes painful sores. A careful examination failed to find any fleas and the two ladies were adamant that the cat did not spend much time grooming itself. I knew from experience that owners are not always observant about this and also that many cats like to groom in secret in their favourite resting places. Apparently there was another cat in the house but it spent most of its life outside. There had been no sign of fleas and therefore no treatment had been given.

'Well, Mrs Evans,' I said for the umpteenth time that day, 'this is a straightforward case of flea allergy.' Both ladies' faces dropped a mile.

'What?' said her friend. 'Are you seriously expecting us to believe that? We haven't seen any fleas and Mona's house is the cleanest you've ever seen!'

'I'm quite sure of it,' I replied. 'But, believe me, I'm quite sure of my diagnosis too!' I spent some time explaining about the life cycle of the flea – how it was spent mainly in the environment and how in allergic cats like Fifi only a few fleas would be enough to cause the problem. I could tell I wasn't getting far – and now I had reached the more difficult bit: how to get the ladies to treat the cats and the home. Spraying was out of the question – Mrs Evans's hands had arthritis and would have trouble holding the cats and spraying even with the help of her friend. And what about the house? This was complicated: Mrs Evans lived in a one-bedroom flat with two main rooms. We agreed that she would ask her home help to spray the carpets and the pets' bedding before she hoovered.

Three weeks later there was no sign of improvement.

In fact, if anything things were worse. I explained that when the weather got colder in the autumn, the fleas would not survive outside and Fifi would get better, and I asked the owners to persevere with the treatment. They sighed and looked despondent, and I heard one lady muttering about having the cat put to sleep. As time passed, though, I forgot all about Fifi – after all, she was one of hundreds of similar cases.

One Monday in late October the ladies were back with an even balder Fifi. This time, however, I caught a flea, much to their consternation. 'That's the first one she's ever had on her,' they said. 'She must have picked it up in here!'

'But she's been in her basket all the time,' I said. 'It isn't possible.' I asked how the spraying had been going and it soon became apparent that the home help had not done any because she suffered from asthma. Furthermore Mrs Evans had been bitten around her ankles – a typical site for flea bites. This made me more determined than ever to solve the problem.

'How do you feel about calling the council in?' I said. This perplexed the two old ladies, who were unaware that the council could help. 'I'm sure that they'll arrange for fumigation, especially now that you've been bitten too.'

Mrs Evans looked doubtful. 'Won't it harm the cats?' she asked.

I reassured her that it wouldn't and gave her the number of the local authority, adding that hundreds of people had availed themselves of this service lately – it had been one of the worst years on record for fleas.

Now I felt confident that we had a reasonable chance

of success with good environmental control in place. Also, vets have many insecticides to choose between with sprays, powders, baths, dips, collars and new drugs that sterilise the female flea. I added, for double reassurance, 'We should be able to come up with something if this doesn't work. There are so many possibilities – we're really spoilt for choice.'

By late November we were beginning at last to see progress. First, the bites on Mrs Evans's ankles had gone and not returned – to me the most conclusive proof of success – and second, we could see a fine stubble of hair returning on Fifi's bald patches. 'I'm very optimistic that all the hair will grow back by Christmas. Just wait and see!' I said. It's never wise to be so confident but I was sure that we had the problem under control – at least until next summer, when it would probably return with the next wave of fleas.

Sure enough just before Christmas my final examination revealed a fine crop of glistening hair. 'She looks lovely!' I said, taking pride in my dermatological skill.

'Yes,' said one lady, with a smile. "We finally found something that helped. A garlic capsule every day has done the trick. I never did believe that fleas had anything to do with it.'

Skin diseases are not restricted to cats and dogs, though, and I found a worrying condition in my next patient, a hamster. These little animals are popular as children's pets and we see a fair few at the hospital. They are easy to care for but when a hamster gets to about two years of age, it is old. Most of our hamster patients are suffering from age-related illnesses. They develop a skin disease caused by the *Demodex* mite, which virtually all animals have and which is present in the skin from soon after birth. It doesn't usually show itself unless the immune system is depressed, generally as a result of old age. This is when the hamster quite commonly develops a cancerous growth.

But Jane's hamster, a three-year-old male and therefore very old, had a common condition more usually seen in young animals. His back end was wet, he had stopped exercising on his wheel and his appetite had gone. Jane looked on anxiously as I examined Fluff gingerly. I am always a bit circumspect when examining hamsters as they can be quite grumpy when they are woken up. They are nocturnal and are sleepy when they come to surgery. A grumpy hamster can – and has done to me many times – inflict a painful bite, which will draw blood. I managed to get Fluff by the scruff of his neck and then had a look at the other end.

'There's not much doubt about the diagnosis, Jane, he's got wet tail,' I said.

Jane was about eleven and had taken time off school – with permission, she was quick to point out – so that she could be with her mum when she came to the hospital. 'I thought that's what it was,' she said, with a tremor in her voice. 'I read about it in my hamster book. Will it mean that he'll have to be put to sleep?'

I had to admit that the outlook was not good. Three is a good age for a hamster, although I have seen the odd one reach its fourth birthday. Wet tail usually carries a poor outlook: it is a form of enteritis – inflammation of the intestines – and probably caused by several things, including bugs, stress and poor conditions, such as those found in some pet shops. In Fluff's case I thought that his age might have something to do with it, which would make a cure unlikely.

I thought for a moment and decided that Jane would be happier if we tried some treatment. 'There's no guarantee that it will work, Jane, but at least we can try. What we must do is get some fluids down Fluff to prevent dehydration, and he'll need antibiotics, which you'll have to give him. Tempt him a little and often with anything he likes to eat.'

I gave Jane a syringe, showed her how to draw up the antibiotic and watched as she successfully got it into Fluff's mouth. One thing was certain: Fluff was going to get very good care – he couldn't have wished for a better nurse. But we would have to wait and see. As they were leaving I had a quick word with Jane's mother and asked her to warn Jane that Fluff might just die and pretty quickly at that.

'Oh, I think she knows – she's very sensible.'

It was a pleasant surprise, then, to see a much rejuvenated Fluff a week later. Jane and her mother had taken it in turns to stay up, giving him fluids round the clock and tempting him to eat, at first with more or less any titbit, but later with his usual hamster food. By day five of the treatment he was improving so much that they no longer had to stay up at night, which was just as well as they were both pretty tired. As Fluff was doing so well, I prescribed another week of antibiotics and said, 'Come back if you're worried – well done!'

I heard nothing more about him until six months

later when I received a nice letter from Jane, saying that Fluff had died in his sleep a few days before and she was grateful for the extra time he had had. She finished by asking what she had to do to become a vet. I smiled to myself: I had been eleven when I decided I wanted to be a vet. I wrote back to her with advice about working hard at school, told her what subjects to study and added, 'You can come and practice with us when you're in college.'

CHAPTER NINE

The Hospital at Night

All veterinary surgeons must provide a twenty-four-hour service. Some large practices set up a rota so that each vet spends some nights on call, while others join up in a group that shares the duty so that each vet gets a reasonable amount of time off. In London and other big cities emergency clinics will see clients at night and return them to their usual vet the next day, so that vets can work a normal day and always sleep well at night.

Although night duty is an integral part of the job and can be a source of great satisfaction, few vets enjoy it.

After the first few years the novelty wears off and you come to realise that night duty means disturbed sleep and that genuine emergencies are rare. It is always best to try to see your vet during the day unless, of course, your pet develops a life-threatening condition after hours.

At the Harmsworth the night duty vet also has to look after the large number of inpatient animals – there may be as many as fifty. Two nurses are on hand during the night to monitor, care for and keep an eye on things. They also assess each emergency as it arrives and call in the vet as necessary and they answer the many phone calls. Sometimes callers are rude and aggressive. Many years ago when working at the Harmsworth for the first time and living in a flat above the hospital, I would stay up and talk to the ambulance drivers and occasionally answer the phones. One night when a driver had a heart attack I had to answer the phones all night and I discovered just how unreasonable a few people could be: one man threatened to 'do me in' when he phoned at four in the morning wanting his dog seen immediately for a limp that it had had for six weeks. Most patients come in before eleven, though, and after that it gets quieter but most vets know that it is hard to sleep well on duty, even if it is quiet. You always have an ear open in case the phone rings – sometimes people telephone after midnight to find out surgery hours!

One of the most amusing calls (in retrospect!) I have had came in when I was in private practice. A frantic owner rang at three in the morning saying that her cat was dying of a heart attack and I must attend immediately. I tried to question her because I needed more information but she hung up in fury. Ten minutes later I spoke to her husband – and I was able to work out that the cat, which was only six months old, was probably in season. She was rolling about 'in agony' and wailing. Furthermore five tom cats were howling outside. I explained that cats don't get heart attacks as we know them and certainly not at six months but the owners insisted that I visit them. When I arrived, just after four, their cat had got out of an open window and disappeared with the tom cats.

A day later I telephoned to make sure she had returned. She had – and she was a lot calmer. I suggested she might be better off spayed as she would almost certainly be pregnant. 'Oh, no!' came the reply. 'We want her to have kittens.' Incidentally, one of the commonest old wives' tales you're likely to hear about animals is that they should be allowed to have one litter before neutering. However, this makes no difference to the dog or cat and it is best to do the operation at six months when the womb is small and easy to remove.

In addition to the normal twenty-four-hour cover by the vets and nurses at the hospital, the RSPCA also provides an emergency ambulance service but it is nowhere near as comprehensive as the human service: there may be an injured cat in north-west London but the ambulance is miles away in the East End. Most emergencies are best transported to the hospital by the owner, which is why the service exists mainly for strays.

A genuine emergency, of course, cannot wait and

any vet just gets out of bed and rushes in. Tom was my first emergency in what turned out to be a busy night. He was an old cat who spent most of his time outside and came in at night to sleep. He had been missing for much of the evening and when he turned up he refused his evening meal. His owner, an elderly lady, wasn't too worried and decided to leave it until the morning.

In the early hours, though, she was woken by anguished cries and furious scrabbling at the litter tray. It was obvious that Tom couldn't relieve himself so the owner rang the RSPCA emergency service. Half an hour later Tom got to the hospital and I was phoned by the duty nurses at 1.30 a.m. Within twenty minutes I was setting up the anaesthetic. The male cat is prone to a blockage of the urethra, the tube from the bladder, because it is narrow. The condition usually affects sluggish, rather fat cats that don't go out much and the blockage is caused by minute stones rather like grit. Some unfortunate cats go undetected for a few days – which hardly bears thinking about as their pain must be excruciating.

I gave Tom an injection into the vein and as he slipped into unconsciousness I set to work to try to unblock the urethra by placing a catheter into the bladder. Easier said than done. Gently I pushed the catheter in bit by bit and kept flushing with Walpole's solution, which helps dissolve the crystalline substance that blocks the urethra. After about half an hour I was finally successful. From then it was a simple matter to siphon all the urine out of the bladder and stitch the catheter in place where it would stay for the next few days. Meanwhile Tom was coming round from his anaesthetic – I could almost feel his relief. The nurse and I set up a drip to help start his kidneys functioning again: production of urine would tell me if he would make it long term.

At 3 a.m. I was ready for bed again – but it wasn't to be. A call came in that a cat had fallen from a balcony and impaled itself on a railing spike. Twenty minutes later the driver brought the poor animal in. It was a terrible sight. He had had to call in the fire brigade, whose officers had cut the railing but had decided wisely to leave the cat on the spike, which had passed through its abdomen. The ambulance driver carefully carried in the cat, a young female of no more than six months. She was in desperate pain so I immediately gave her an intravenous anaesthetic and started to free her from the spike. She didn't look as though she had lost much blood so I thought that nothing major had been penetrated although I had to check her intestines.

First we set up a drip then eased out the spike. Then I prepared her for an exploratory laparotomy, an operation in which the abdomen is opened, so that I could see what damage there was inside. Surprisingly only a couple of holes had to be patched up. Half an hour later I was finished. While I was writing up her card I noticed her name – Lucky.

Four a.m. It was hardly worth going to bed but I drove home anyway feeling weary. I seemed to be the only person about. I fell asleep almost instantly and then it was 7 a.m., time to get up, have some breakfast and go back to work. It was hard to get out of bed but I was anxious to see how my patients were faring.

It had all been worth it. Tom was sitting up, purring

and making friendly overtures to the nurses, and Lucky had passed a couple of peaceful hours free from pain and seemed remarkably bright. So far so good, but I knew that with her peritonitis was still a real danger: it often occurs with penetrating wounds of the abdomen. By 5.30 I had had it, and went home. When things go well it is all worthwhile, but I needed a couple of early nights to recover. Thank heavens nights like that are not too common!

Four days later, though, problems set in. Lucky had been doing quite well and had shown interest in food although she hadn't eaten anything. Now she seemed in pain – she resented me touching her tummy – and was running a temperature. I took a blood sample to check her white cell count – a reliable indicator as to whether or not infection has set in. Sure enough, it was sky high. Back she went on to a drip and I prescribed twice daily injections of cephalexin, the most powerful antibiotic at our disposal. Now she had to have really intensive nursing: temperature checks four times daily round the clock, injections, fluids into the vein and lots of tempting with food. After a week I began to despair, she had lost so much weight.

Then Lucky's temperature came down to normal and she seemed to have less pain in her abdomen. I decided to try an old ruse I had learned years ago and one we still use from time to time. A gave Lucky a small injection of Valium and offered her some pilchards – her favourite – immediately afterwards. From then on Lucky took a little food each day, in gradually increasing amounts. A bonus was that she could have her antibiotics in her food instead of in the twice daily injections, which she was beginning to hate.

Three weeks after her accident she was fit enough to go home and there she made rapid progress. The balcony was out of bounds. I explained to the owners that although we rarely see a cat that has fallen off a balcony twice, it has happened and there is no guarantee that an animal will learn from its mistakes.

Some emergencies are life threatening but quickly resolved. Generally, cats are fastidious eaters and we don't often see poisoning in them but this general rule does not apply to kittens and cats under a year old – the age at which they start to grow up. If a kitten's mouth is painful or it has difficulty in eating I am always alerted to a possible foreign body. Any refusal in a kitten to eat must be taken seriously since when healthy they will normally eat voraciously.

In Spud's case there was never any doubt that he had eaten a foreign body because he was gagging and choking and a piece of thread was hanging from his mouth. His owner had been sewing on the evening he was presented to the emergency service. Fortunately Miss Gordon had had the presence of mind not to tug on the thread: it might have been stuck round something important like the larynx or still attached to the needle. An X-ray showed a long needle lodged in the upper part of Spud's gullet – it couldn't be seen by looking down the cat's throat. Spud needed a general anaesthetic so that I could fish it out – not without a little risk since he was only eight weeks old.

He was already fairly sedated so I knocked him right out with a little anaesthetic gas, called Halothane, which we gave him through a tight-fitting mask. He struggled a bit and I knew how he felt: I can remember being given gas and air as a youngster when I turned up at Casualty with broken limbs and cuts and bruises. (I was forever having accidents, an unfortunate tendency that – touch wood – disappeared in my thirties.) Being gassed down is not pleasant but it is safe and recovery is quick.

A few minutes later I was examining Spud's larynx and could see the needle. I had to cut it in half with pin cutters, which made it easy to remove. The thread had looped around the entrance to the larynx and I dealt with this in the same way by cutting it in several places. The whole procedure took less than five minutes and five minutes after that Spud came round, albeit looking a bit sleepy. He was also hungry, judging by the noise he was making, and I was happy to let him home for the night. If only all emergencies could be so satisfactorily resolved!

Some of the more complicated situations involve the owners and the police. One emergency of which I have seen quite a few examples at the Harmsworth, involves injury to dogs inflicted by their owners or other humans – burglars, for instance. Occasionally the dog gets involved in a serious domestic dispute and invariably the police are called in. One Saturday a relatively peaceful evening was broken by the arrival of a police van and an almost hysterical young woman. With them was her Doberman with a large sheet tied round him. A lot of blood was oozing through it.

'He's been stabbed,' said one policeman, while his colleague tried to console the dog's owner, who had a swollen lip and a black eye. Earlier in the evening the woman and her boyfriend had had an argument, which had led to physical violence. The dog had leapt to the defence of the woman and bitten her boyfriend, who had responded by stabbing the dog in the back several times, causing it to let go and collapse on the floor. The screaming had alerted the neighbours, who had called the police – which was just as well for Prince as almost immediately he was on his way to hospital. The policemen had used the sheet as an impromptu bandage. Prince's attacker had been taken by ambulance to the local hospital so that his bites could be dressed.

Prince's wounds were not as serious as the amount of blood suggested. He required an immediate anaesthetic, a drip and half a dozen stitches in each wound and a new bandage. An hour later he was starting to come round and looked a lot better. In theory he would be discharged the next day but I was reluctant to send him home if the boyfriend was going to be around. Prince's owner was still waiting for news so I had a chat with her. She assured me that she never wanted to see the man again and she would be getting a court order to prevent him from coming anywhere near her. The police would prosecute him if she would testify against him, but it might be difficult to persuade the magistrate that the injuries inflicted on the dog were unreasonable as the man acted in self-defence. It would depend on how the story was portrayed in court by the defence solicitors.

A few days later Prince went home, healing well. While he had been in hospital his owner had visited him and he had responded with excited yelps and furious wags of his tail. He was obviously well loved and would be well cared-for. I left the prosecution side of the case to the professionals and hoped that common sense would prevail and that Prince could live in a peaceful house.

Some of our consistently busiest nights on call are during the run-up to Bonfire Night. A few years ago there was only one night of problems but now the animals have to put up with weeks of trouble. It starts in October when bangers are let off late at night, frightening dogs and cats. The emergency service often gets calls from distraught owners. As 5 November approaches, the noise gets worse and we find ourselves dispensing tranquillisers widely. Dogs and cats vary in their response to the loud bangs: some dogs have trembling fits, others howl or bark, go off their food and refuse to go out for walks. Cats get lost and ward seven is usually overcrowded. Don't forget to keep your animals inside as much as possible at this time of year and to try to drown the noise with the radio or television.

Bonfires are hazardous to wildlife. Hedgehogs in particular are prone to hiding under them with disastrous consequences when they are lit. Over the years I have seen many casualties associated with fireworks and two instances stick in my mind, one a dog the other a cat, and they came in at the same time.

It was 5 November and he was a dark-coated dog, difficult to see as he wandered along London's East End streets late at night, possibly on his way home. It was busy with late-night traffic speeding along. The incessant bangs and crashes didn't seem to worry him –

perhaps because he was a latch-key street-wise dog let out to fend for himself when his owners were not at home. Maybe on that particular night this dog's owners were at a party or in the pub. They probably thought that he could look after himself. They were wrong.

A passer-by saw what happened next. A group of youths yelled at the dog and he barked at them. One produced a banger, lit it, waited until the last possible moment and threw it at the dog. As it landed at his feet it went off and, with a scream that brought laughter from the gang, he raced across the road. Unluckily for him a car was speeding past and caught him in the head and front legs. The dog was tossed in the air and landed in the gutter. The car screeched to a halt and the driver saw the youths run off. They were never identified.

The driver, a young man, went over to the gutter where the dog was lying. At first he thought it was dead and there was a pool of blood by its head, but on closer inspection he could see its chest rising and falling and he could hear it whimpering although its eyes were closed and it seemed unconscious. The cars continued to speed by. Fortunately the young man had a mobile phone. He rang the police, who contacted the RSPCA. As luck would have it an ambulance was not far away.

Twenty minutes later the ambulance driver was checking over the dog before moving him. He was very shocked: the mucous membranes of his mouth were a pale grey-pink and his breathing was shallow. The only obvious injury was a severely broken front leg but the dog was bleeding from his mouth. All that could be done was to get him to the hospital. The ambulance driver rolled the dog carefully on to a blanket and then, with the help of the young man, gently lifted him into the ambulance, using the corners of the blanket. Meanwhile, the young man was feeling distinctly shaky. The ambulance driver advised him to report the accident to the police, as the law requires, and go home. The Harmsworth would keep him informed of the dog's progress. Then the driver set off with an estimated twenty-minute journey ahead of him.

When I heard about the accident it was quite late and I had been about to set off for home. The duty nurses set up the theatre in case we needed to operate and the X-ray developing machine was switched on again. We sat down with a cup of tea to wait. A few minutes later the driver arrived. The patient had taken a turn for the worse. He had partially regained consciousness and was screaming in pain, which was distressing to see as we lifted him into the preparation room.

In recent years pain relief for animals has improved immeasurably and after an injection the dog became calmer and more manageable. A drip was set up to counteract shock and I started to check him out to find out where the injuries were. The most obvious was the swinging front leg. No doubt about that one: his radius and ulna, the two main bones below the elbow, were badly broken. I put the leg in a support splint. Almost immediately I could sense the dog's relief: broken bones are very painful, especially when they rub together, and splinting gives stability and ends the pain. With a little help he was able to stand and I could see that his other legs were not injured. His heart and lungs sounded surprisingly strong – no sign of any bleeding into the lungs. Finally I checked his mouth and found a broken tooth and a broken jaw. Poor dog – no wonder he had been crying out in pain. Fortunately the jaw wasn't badly broken and a simple suture round the main canine teeth would stabilise it.

The next morning the dog was fit enough for a general anaesthetic and X-ray. First I repaired his jaw, then took the X-ray. His radius and ulna had been smashed to smithereens. There was no possibility of fixing it internally with plates and screws so I changed the splint to a full plaster-of-paris support, keeping my fingers crossed that the leg would heal. He was a young dog, and nature works miracles in the young. His immediate prospects were good – but would his owners come forward and, if not, would we be able to home him? His temperament had improved after I had stabilised his injuries – while I was examining him when he first came in he had tried to bite me, and had been especially touchy about his back end. He was probably bruised there, although I couldn't find any obvious injury. For the next week he would be in the care of the nurses while we decided what to do with him.

Meanwhile I turned my attention to a young black and white female cat, who had been rushed in not long after the dog. She had been caught in a fire in the small flat where she lived with her owner, an old man. Although the fire brigade had been on the scene quickly, the old man was dead, and his cat had been found unconscious in the bathroom. Paramedics pulled her round with oxygen and brought her in to us.

We see a lot of cats rescued from house fires and this one was typical. She smelt terribly of burning hair and smoke, and was having trouble breathing. We put her into an oxygen cage and gave her high doses of steroids to counteract the inflammation in the lungs that smoke inhalation invariably causes, and antibiotics. If the lungs have been damaged these cases usually get worse after three or four days but as I was checking her I was pleased with her progress: her breathing was apparently normal although she showed no interest in food and cowered in the back of the cage. It had all been a shocking experience for her – losing her owner, the fire, being rescued, resuscitated and now finding herself in this strange place. What was worse, she was having to receive twice daily injections.

By the end of the week she was holding her own – still not eating but with no obvious lung problems, which an X-ray confirmed. The cat owed her life to the skill of the paramedic who had revived her as much as our intensive treatment.

Meanwhile the dog had attracted the attention of millions of viewers, most of whom wanted to adopt him. This was heart-warming but we would have to select his new owners carefully. It is not easy to take on a dog with this one's history. His previous owner wouldn't have trained him properly, he might have vices, like biting the postman or chasing bicycles, and was used to a life of roaming the streets getting into mischief. This would have to be trained out of him and would need lots of patience. There was also the smashed front leg. It was quite possible that it would not heal and either extensive surgery or, more likely, amputation would be necessary.

Two weeks after the accident I was going over these points with Mr and Mrs Page who live on the outskirts of London. They had a splendid home to offer the dog, with a garden and someone around all day. I kept my fingers crossed as they left with him and made an appointment to change the plaster-of-paris a fortnight later. This would be the crunch time as far as the leg was concerned because if it wasn't showing any sign of healing by then, it probably wouldn't.

In the event Cracker, as he had been renamed, came stomping into the surgery, using his bad leg, a very good sign. On X-ray, it still looked a bit of a mess, but it felt firm and a strong callus was forming. I replaced the plaster-of-paris, and while he was under the anaesthetic I castrated and microchipped him. From then on Cracker never looked back, and the patient loving care of his owners has been rewarded by an extrovert, lively, well-adjusted dog – and you can't tell which was the injured leg.

At about the same time that Cracker was going to his new home, the paramedic who had revived the little cat had phoned in to see how she was. He had been chatting with his wife and they had decided that they would like to adopt her. It was the perfect end to her story. She had regained her confidence, made a full recovery and was eating us out of house and home, and we all felt happy for her and her new family as she left the hospital for better times. It's one of the great joys of the job when an animal makes a 100 per cent recovery against all the odds.

EPILOGUE

Looking back over the last few years since the television cameras arrived, I am struck how little some things change. Cats still fall off balconies, dogs still get involved in accidents, and there are always plenty of strays. But I do feel that in some areas the problems are fewer and that perhaps the animal-welfare messages constantly put out by the RSPCA are getting through. Certainly having the television cameras around has helped and I am optimistic that animals will benefit from increased public awareness of animal-welfare issues.

Even after four years of filming, the ingredients that make up an interesting programme still mystify me. Long ago I realised that the creation of a television programme is a skilful affair and that the producers and researchers view things from a perspective totally different from mine since I'm always immersed in the technical and scientific aspect of my work. Quite early on in filming I realised I should leave the selection of cases to the television professionals. One day producers were short of a story to balance the week's programme and I was joined half-way through my ward round by Veronica, a researcher. It was her job to talk to clients, vets and generally look round the hospital to see what was going on with an eye for a good story. The programme still lacked a light story, preferably involving a cat as plenty of dogs were already 'in the can'.

'What have you got?' Veronica asked me.

I wracked my brains. 'Not a lot. The usual RTAs, a pyo, half a dozen stray cats. We've still got ward seven to look at.'

We trudged out the back through a penetrating drizzle into the warmth of ward seven. A quick look here didn't show anything very interesting as far as I could see. Veronica pointed to a sad-looking kitten in one of the top cages. 'What's wrong with this one?' The kitten had looked oily, with shiny sticky hair, like a fifties pop star. Bits of fur stuck out in spikes and the effect was rather strange.

'Oh,' I said, 'that poor little chap came in last night. He's fallen in some leg wax.'

'Leg wax?' Veronica couldn't believe her ears. 'How did he manage that?'

'It's easy if you're a kitten,' I replied. 'Don't you know that curiosity killed the cat? And they start early!' I didn't want to expose my ignorance: until that night I hadn't even been aware of the existence of leg wax or its purpose. Fortunately it doesn't get to very high temperatures, or at least it hadn't in this case, so there was no danger of burns, although I hadn't known that at first and had come in to see the kitten as an emergency. The owner had been preparing the wax in a small dish when the kitten jumped right into it. After a few unsuccessful attempts late at night to try to remove the wax I had resolved to leave it until the morning. The nurses put a little collar on to stop him trying to remove it himself and he had to go without his supper, hence his sad expression.

'I haven't worked out what to do about it yet,' I told Veronica. But she was already on the radio to the producers in the control room. Here was their case! A quarter of an hour later the whole paraphernalia of film-making was being set up. The cameras arrived, a radio microphone was placed on me by the sound-man, extra lighting was set up, and Rolf arrived full of curiosity as to what could be done. He knew as much about leg wax as me!

In the end I found that a little surgical spirit and gentle rubbing and brushing, with scissors for the worst bits, did the trick. Rolf held the kitten, while I got rid of the wax, bit by bit. The whole thing took about an hour. My first and only leg-wax case. Later the story was edited down to a few minutes and went out in the programme that week. It was an amusing piece and all the nicer because the little kitten made a full recovery. I received dozens of letters advising me on all sorts of substances to get rid of leg wax in any future case.

Even when we're not filming, the series remains on my mind. As I came in one morning and greeted the first half-dozen clients of the day, all waiting for their pets to be admitted, I found myself glancing at their animals while I collected the post. There was the usual variety. An old Labrador with a head tilt – probably a stroke and coming in for symptomatic treatment. That's a good case – and so was the cat next to him, being admitted for an operation on a cauliflower ear. A budgie was egg bound, and a small heavily pregnant crossbreed dog was supposed to have given birth to her pups a week ago. A bitch was in for spaying, and finally we had a gerbil with a cancerous growth. Pity the cameras aren't here, I thought. We've got some interesting cases in today – and these are only the first half-dozen! But as I write there are still four months to go before we start another series, and we will have to wait and see what it brings. That's the fun of it, I simply don't know until the first animal is filmed what will happen, although on reflection that's true of our Animal Hospital all the time. One thing is certain: we won't have time to be bored!

INDEX